INTERNATIONAL MARIJUANA

2018 Edition

The No B.S. Guide to Investing in Weed Stocks Globally

Profit from the legalization of Cannabis in

Canada, Australia, Israel, Europe, U.S. and More

Written by Peter Hatcher, PFA

Limit of Liability/Disclaimer; While the author has used his best efforts in preparing a factually accurate book, he makes no representations or warranties with respect to the accuracy or completeness of its contents. In addition, the advice contained in this book may not be suitable for your situation. The author shall not be liable for any loss of profit or any other commercial damages, including but not limited to special, incidental, consequential, or other damages.

In regard to the stock examples in this book, remember that past performance is no guarantee of success.

Table of Contents

Introduction

Wouldn't it have been nice to own shares of Anheuser-Busch in the 1930's just after prohibition was repealed? Even since 1997, its share price has increased a full 1000% to well over $100 per share. That doesn't even consider its stock splits. This global company now has a market share of nearly 50% in the U.S. alone.

Well now there's an opportunity to own the Anheuser-Busch of the future.

As most people know, millions of investors are already reaping stock market profits in a fast-emerging industry still at ground zero-- the Cannabis industry. *Newsmax* quoted an analyst saying that the "Medical Marijuana industry is projected to Top $40 billion dollars by 2020" in the U.S.

Unfortunately, in the United States, marijuana is still classified as a "Schedule 1" drug on par with heroin and LSD. Consequently, expansion for companies will be difficult. Therefore, the next Anheuser-Busch will likely not be in the U.S. It will be abroad!

The U.S. is one of at least 20 countries on the path to legalization. In fact, there are countries legalizing recreational Marijuana within the next 12 months and their stocks are already exploding. Right this instant, several of these publicly traded companies are tracking to be the next Anheuser-Busch. For all these reasons, millions of Investors are turning to foreign companies all around the world.

For instance, a report from the University of Sydney stated the initial demand for medical cannabis in Australia could be worth more than $100 M a year. This is expected to expand to $300 M a year should recreational cannabis become legal as well. In addition, at the time of this writing, marijuana stocks have dominated the trading on Canada's TSX Venture index, averaging around 10 per cent of the volume on the total exchange!

Did you know you can buy shares of these companies too, regardless of physical location and citizenship? You don't have to be an insider. This book will teach you how!

The following pages are a direct, no-nonsense guide to making easy profit by investing in these global companies. Some of what you'll learn includes:

-A guide on how to choose an online brokerage firm that allows you to buy international stocks cheaply.

-20 countries that just legalized cannabis or are legalizing soon.

-The 20 best, safest, fastest growing marijuana related companies trading on public exchanges around the world. Based on their management, partnerships, contracts and spreadsheets, these companies are most likely to compete for global market share.

-A guide on how to do further research on the selected companies in this book and future companies that have yet to enter the market.

-Trading strategy tips including position trading, swing trading, entry and exit points, margin trading and more.

-Online resources and more!

Around the world, cannabis may become as common as getting prescription medicine in the next five years. In the next ten years, it may become as common as a bottle of wine. Therefore make sure you study the material in this book. Get your ticket to the "International Green Rush" before it's too late!

Getting Started

Before we get into the nitty gritty, let me first say this book already assumes you have experience as a stock trader. Experienced stock traders understand there is no such thing as winning trades 100% of the time. It cannot be done. And this is especially true when investing in stocks growing within an industry just now becoming legal.

Why? These stocks are thinly traded. Therefore, they can be quite volatile.

However, the good news is volatility can be extremely profitable-- especially within an emerging industry such as this one. And with an industry such as this one, if you are patient and you properly diversify your capital within several of the different stocks mentioned later, the chances of seeing considerable returns is definitely in your favor. Companies that can successfully make the leap from penny to a blue chip stock are rare, but savvy investors have already managed to rake in gains of over 1,000% within a few years with stocks like Canadian Marijuana producer, Aurora Cannabis.

If you're looking for modest returns like 3%, it would be better for you to buy an ETF that tracks the S&P 500. However, at the time of this writing, you're better off throwing your cash out the window. Most of the stocks included in this index are overvalued and have been up-trending for the last 8 years with little room left to go. A correction has been long over-do. If you want explosive returns, the strategy should be to buy stocks with enormous potential and upside.

At the time of this writing, most marijuana stocks are penny stocks. This is not necessarily because the companies are terribly run (although some may be), but because the cannabis industry is in its infancy-- and just now becoming legal. The friction between federal illegality and the state legality means uncharted waters. The Nasdaq and the New York Stock Exchange want nearly no part of this until the friction ends. Therefore, to get access to capital, these companies have used reverse mergers and other mechanisms to end up being publicly traded on the over-the-counter exchanges.

OTC exchanges are not taken as seriously as the bigger exchanges. While exchanges like NYSE are tough on quality, OTC generally allows for a greater degree of latitude for the companies that trade on them. As a result, solid marijuana companies like Terra Tech Corp. (TRTC) and mCig Inc. (MCIG) probably shouldn't be on the OTC exchanges. They got there because entrepreneurs thought it was the only way they could get access to capital. After all, with federal illegality still a reality, even a bank loan is nearly impossible.

This is also true in other countries with their own version of OTC exchanges. However, once the U.S. and other countries legalize medical and recreational pot across the board and real earnings start pouring in, it can mean double, triple, or even 10x the profit for these stocks within a few years.

Don't forget, since these stocks are often thinly traded, diversification and risk management are key. For those of you not as equipped with experience in stock trading, this book also contains time-tested stock trading tips and guidelines in subsequent chapters for your quick and easy reference. These useful tips are not at all revolutionary. However, they are often missed as traders let their emotions rule their decisions.

Cannabis 101

Overview

Before plunging head first into marijuana stocks, it is prudent to understand the ins and outs of the industry as well as the plant itself. Each of these companies have products and services related to different aspects of cannabis. While one company may be a producer that grows and sells cannabis, another company may function by leasing the real estate the producer operates on. To make wise investment choices, an investor should know everything there is to know about cannabis. If you are already well-versed, by all means skip to whatever chapter you are ready for.

Cannabis and Cannabinoids

Taken and prepared from the cannabis plant, cannabis is also referred to as 'marijuana' or 'weed'. The most well-known psychoactive part of cannabis, known to make people feel "stoned", is tetrahydrocannabinol (THC); one of 65 other cannabinoids. Cannabinoids are any of a group of closely related compounds found in cannabis that include cannabidiol (CBD).

As more scientific research is conducted involving cannabis and its ability to be used as a medicine, interest in CBD has grown exponentially. CBD does not make people feel "stoned" and actually counters some of the effects of THC. After decades of only high-THC marijuana being available, CBD-rich strains are now being grown for patients. CBD has been featured on numerous forms of media and publications showing how well it works in treating people. It is what ultimately led Mexico to pass recent legislation allowing marijuana for their patients who suffer from severe epilepsy.

Cannabis is intended for use as a drug or medicine in various forms, including smoking, food, through an inhaler, vaporization, etc. Whether it's for medicinal purposes or not, Cannabis users feel its effects within minutes when smoked, but longer when eaten. Included among these effects are a heightened mood, an altered change in perception and an increase in appetite. Short term side effects may include short-term memory issues, cottonmouth, impaired motor skills and feelings of paranoia. (Leafly.com)

Various forms of Consumption

Cannabis is consumed in the following ways:

1. Smoking, which usually involves burning the cannabinoids and then inhaling vaporized cannabinoids through a small pipes or bong.

2. Tea, typically in which a mixture of cannabis is infused with fat (e.g., coconut oil, cream or butter) combined with tea leaves and water to make a chai or latte-type drink. You can even consider dissolving cannabutter into a cup of tea or coffee. These drinks have little to no psychoactive effects.

3. Edibles, in which cannabis or cannabis oils are infused into baked food items such as brownies and cookies. Because of the slow, tedious digestive process, edibles take much longer to kick in. However, they can have more intense psychoactive effects.

4. Vaporizer, a device used to heat up marijuana buds (around 390-something degrees F) to the point where the material (including the THC, Cbd/cbn, etc.) evaporates into a vapor form. Typically, the vapor is drawn in slower and held for longer than smoke, somewhere between 15-30 seconds. Its chemical compounds vaporize at a much lower, less harmful temperature. The taste of vaporized cannabis is often preferred to that of combusted flower. In addition, the vapor is much easier on the lungs.

5. Ingestible Oils, basically any cannabis concentrate that is taken orally. They can induce delayed, yet powerful effects much like edibles. They mostly come in capsules to be consumed with food and a drink.

6. Topicals, in which lotions and balms are infused with a mixture of cannabis. Thereafter, they can be applied directly to the skin for localized relief of pain or inflammation without psychoactive effects.

Varieties

According to the United Nations Office on Drugs and Crime (UNODC), "the amount of THC present in a cannabis sample is generally used as a measure of cannabis potency." The three main forms of cannabis products are the flower, resin (hashish), and oil (hash oil).

1. Marijuana

Marijuana consists of the dried flower buds and leaves of the female Cannabis plant. This is the most popular form of consumption, containing 3% to 20% THC, with reports of up-to 33% THC.

2. Kief

Those small, sticky crystals that cover cannabis flower buds. Kief is the powder, rich in trichomes, which can accumulate in containers or be sifted from the leaves and flowers of cannabis plants. Trichomes keep away hungry animals by producing disorientation. Kief can either be consumed in powder form or compressed to produce cakes of hashish.

3. Hashish

Hashish is a concentrated resin cake or ball produced from compressed kief. It may also be produced by scraping the resin from the surface of the cannabis plant and rolling it into a ball. It can be consumed orally, smoked or vaporized.

4. Tincture

A solution of alcohol containing cannabinoids extracted from the cannabis plant. It is often referred to as "green dragon". The tincture is typically made by soaking the dried flower buds in ethanol and evaporating the solvent. The THC and other cannabinoids dissolve into the alcohol. The tincture is ordinarily consumed orally, but may also be applied to the skin.

5. Hash oil

It's the extracted oil from the Cannabis plant by solvent extraction, formed into a hardened or viscous mass. To make the oil, you grind up the pot, flush it with the solvent, then heat it and pressurize it to release the oil. The end product can have a consistency that ranges from that of olive oil to a hard and brittle toothpaste. Hash oil can be the most potent of the main cannabis products because of its high level of THC. The drug can be smoked or vaporized directly, or used to make edible products or balms.

6. Infusions

There are many varieties of cannabis infusions. The plant material is mixed with the solvent (such as dairy butter, cooking oil, ointments, etc) and then pressed and filtered to express the oils of the plant into the solvent. Cannabis is being infused in numerous products these days such as teas, cooking oils, massage oils, ointments and of course various edibles. More than ever, the list of products continues to grow.

The Cannabis Strains: Sativa vs. Indica

Indica and Sativa are the two major types of cannabis plants. They can be mixed together to create hybrid strains. Each strain has its own range of effects on the body and mind, resulting in a wide range of medicinal benefits. Indica strains tend to be more psychoactive. They are physically sedating, perfect for relaxing before going to bed or watching a movie. With Sativa, a well-being, cerebral uplifting and ease is often associated. This makes them ideal for social gatherings and creative projects. (Leafly.com)

A patient suffering from fatigue or depression may use Sativa during the day. A different patient being treated for inflammation or insomnia, will likely choose an Indica strain at night. Most Indica varieties come from central Asia and the Indian subcontinent, while Sativa generally originates in the equatorial regions, such as Thailand and Mexico.

Visit the Marijuana Strain Explorer at Leafly.com, to see a list of the most popular versions of these cannabis strains. These include everything from girl scout cookies, Bubba Kush, Pineapple Express, Amnesia Haze and more.

Choosing an International Online Brokerage

Smoking weed may be a pastime for some; but strides in medical marijuana research for countless diseases are causing FDA approvals to increase yearly. As the legalization of cannabinoids, THC, CBD and marijuana becomes more of a reality, millions of retail investors will continue to pour their money into the marijuana market. Short of starting your own company, it is likely better to invest in the stocks of viable cannabis related companies to get a piece of the billion dollar pie. The first step is selecting a brokerage firm in which you can trade international stocks cheaply.

Technology is making investing in stocks overseas cheaper and easier than ever before. Fortunately for us, we no longer have to leave our international stocks in the costly hands of institutional managers.

There are different ways to trade foreign stocks:

American Depositary Receipt (ADR)

Introduced to the financial markets in 1927, an American depositary receipt (ADR) is a stock that trades in the U.S. but represents a specified number of shares in a foreign company. Issued by banks and brokers, ADRs are bought and sold on American public exchanges just like regular stocks. FInancial institutions price an ADR high enough to show substantial value, yet low enough to make it affordable for individual investors.

There are three different types of ADR issues. The most basic type of ADR represents foreign companies that don't qualify or don't wish to have their ADR listed on an exchange. They are found on the over-the-counter market and are an easy and inexpensive way to gauge interest for its securities in North America. Since they trade thinly, most international cannabis stocks found on U.S. exchanges will fall in this category.

Non-ADR Stocks

To get your hands on a Non-ADR foreign stock or ORDs (ordinary shares), you have to have a broker that can convert dollars into a foreign currency. In addition, sometimes you have to pay another small fee to cover brokerage costs on a foreign exchange. The ordinary shares of foreign-based companies are not always officially listed on U.S. market exchanges. However, you can trade ORD stocks or trade funds that invest in ORD stocks through most of the brokers listed below.

Top 4 Brokerage Firms for International Trading

Many online brokers, like Ally.com do not offer either ADR or Non-ADR securities for trading on their platforms. The best way to trade these stocks are through foreign-trading services offered by quality online firms like International Brokers, Fidelity Investments, Charles Schwab & Co and a few others. Determining which of these brokers has the better deal for you depends on how large is the amount of capital you will be trading with, the size of your transactions and how often you will be trading.

Furthermore, each of these brokers offer trading on margin. The amount of money you can borrow on margin toward the purchase of stocks is typically limited to 50 percent of the value of marginable securities in your account. However, it is prudent to borrow less to lower your risk. Once you borrow on margin, you are required to maintain a certain amount of value in your account, depending on the diversity of the securities you possess. Typically, the equity maintenance requirement is at least 30% of the total account value. Brokers calculate your buying power and cash available for withdrawal.

1. Interactive Brokers LLC.

Due to its transparency and its low costs, this broker is a top pick for professional traders. Lower commissions, no ticket charges; no minimums; no software, platform, or reporting fees; and extremely low financing rates.

Trade Execution

IB offers great, quick execution of trades. Most brokers trade against your orders or sell them to others to execute who will trade against them. The resulting poor execution can result in costs higher than the commission you pay. IB continuously searches and reroutes to the best available prices for stocks and options. (interactivebrokers.com)

Stock Yield Enhancement

There's even a way to safely make extra income through their Stock Yield Enhancement Program. The program lets them borrow shares in exchange for cash collateral, and then lends the shares to traders who are willing to pay a fee to borrow them. You will be paid a loan fee each day that your stock is on loan.

Foreign Stocks

Most importantly, IB offers ADR stocks and non-ADR stocks. You can literally trade on over 100 market centers in 24 countries. You'll have direct market access to stocks, options, futures, forex, bonds, ETFs and CFDs from a single universal account. You can fund your account in multiple currencies and trade assets denominated in multiple currencies from a single account.

Fees

Interactive Brokers differs from many other online brokerages by offering a trading fee structure based on the number of shares traded. Other brokerages, like the ones mentioned later in this chapter, have a flat fee. Interactive Brokers charges $0.0050 per share traded. That's great if you are buying less than a 1,000 shares. For instance, for a transaction of 250 shares, IB will only charge $1.25! However, if you plan on trading at a high volume, it may be better to go with a flat fee brokerage.

Margin Rates

If you're looking to trade on margin, you will love the rates IB offers. They are extremely low. The maximum margin rate is the benchmark rate plus 1.5%. This blended rate is based on account balance. Larger cash balances receive increasingly better rates. For balances of $100,000 or less, the margin rate is currently only 2.16%! It only gets lower from there.

Minimums

Interactive Brokers is able to maintain such low rates and fees because it requires a minimum of $10,000 to open an account with them. They make their money through the volume of activity of each customer. For those of you who do not have the funds for such a deposit, this may be a deal breaker. However, if you do have the funds, you'll save big on costs in the long run. To maintain the account thereafter, you must maintain at least $2,000 or non-USD equivalent in your account. Otherwise, fees may be collected.

For more current information, visit their website: interactivebrokers.com

2. Fidelity Investments

Fidelity is another great broker for trading foreign stocks. It is especially great for traders who want to keep a portion of their capital parked in a specific foreign currency for several years. You will pay the conversion rate, but low brokerage commissions.

For instance, after Fidelity turns your currency into Euros, you'll be able to do online trades in market exchanges of France, Germany, Belgium, etc. As with Interactive Brokers, all dividends received by you would remain in euros and your Fidelity account would show separate U.S. dollar and foreign currency credit balances.

Fees

In response to the growing competition, Fidelity lowered its commissions in February 2017, dropping from $7.95 per trade to $4.95. While not as low as IB, that's actually near the bottom among quality online brokers, especially considering the level of excellence the company's customer service provides.

Margin Rates

Fidelity offers relatively low margin rates. Like IB, the margin rate you pay depends on your outstanding margin balance. The higher your balance, the lower the margin rate you are charged. For balances between $0-$24,999, the margin rate is Base + 1.50%-- which at the time of this writing, translates to an effective rate of 8.325%. With balances of $25,000-$49,999, the effective rate is 7.825%. Between $50,000-$99,999, the rate is 6.875% and so on.

Minimums

At the time of this writing, Fidelity has a minimum investment of $2,500 for brokerage accounts. that's fairly high compared with other online brokers. For IRA accounts, the minimum is $0. If you want to invest in mutual funds, most Fidelity and non-Fidelity funds carry a $2,500 minimum as well.

For more information (like current rates and fees), visit their website: www.fidelity.com.

3. Charles Schwab & Co.

Charles Schwab offers plenty of trading and educational features that many newbies will find useful. Schwab has extensive research tools at your fingertips and 24/7 customer service. Furthermore, customers who already possess a Schwab bank account or an OptionsXpress account can access all accounts through a single log-in.

Fees

Like Interactive Brokers and Fidelity, Charles Schwab is ahead of most of its competitors with a $4.95 flat-rate for stock trades. The same goes for option trades, which run at $4.95, plus $.65 per contract. Investors trading ETFs will also enjoy Schwab as the leading broker in its offering of 229 commission-free ETFs. Interestingly, Schwab offers to refund fees or commission if for any reason you're not completely satisfied.

For foreign stocks, you pay a single fee covering both its brokerage commission and the currency conversion. However, there is an additional fee for the overseas broker. Schwab's fee is 0.5%, with a $100 minimum on trades smaller than $20,000. The overseas fee ranges from 0.4% to 1.2%.

Margin Rates

Schwab's low margin rates are comparable to Fidelity. For balances between $0-$24,999, the current margin rate is 8.50%. With balances of $25,000-$49,999, the effective rate is 8.00%. Between $50,000-$99,999, the rate is 7.00% and so on. To begin borrowing at Schwab, you must have at least $5,000 in cash or marginable securities in your account.

Minimums

To open an account with Schwab, the minimum deposit is $1,000. This minimum is waived if you set up an automatic monthly transfer of $100 through direct deposit or Schwab MoneyLink® or open a Schwab Bank High Yield Investor Checking® account linked to your brokerage account.

For more information (like current rates and fees), visit their website: www.schwab.com.

4. Scottrade, Inc.

At mostly only $7 per trade, Scottrade also offers access to foreign stocks from over 20 countries. Like the brokers mentioned earlier, Scottrade provides customers the ability to trade international equities alongside domestic equities via one central account.

Foreign Stocks

Scottrade provides customers with advanced research and trading tools to help you manage investments intelligently and on your own terms.

Scottrade offers ADRs for companies in over 20 countries throughout Europe, Africa, South America, and Asia Pacific. Through an online trading account, you can use the stock screener to get online quotes and explore ADR stocks or ORDs that you can use to expand your portfolio's investments internationally. In addition, you can start your research online with news, charts and stock information for many international stocks, available free of charge with your Scottrade account.

Fees

For customers at Scottrade, most array of products and services to help meet financial goals, are provided at no cost. Their trading fees and commissions are intentionally straightforward and clear. Lastly, they don't charge clients fees for account maintenance or inactivity. At the time of this writing, an online trade is only $7. If broker assisted, the fee is $32.

Margin Rates

During the time your loan is outstanding, Scottrade charges interest daily based on the amount of funds you borrow. Keeping a higher debit balance in your account generally makes you eligible for lower interest rates. For instance, at the time of this writing, a loan balance under $9,999.99 results in an interest rate of 8.25% (Base Rate + 1.25%). Between $10,000 and $24,999.99, the interest rate is 8%.

An initial deposit of $2,000 is required to request margin privileges. Once a loan is extended, you're required to keep a minimum equity level, called the maintenance requirement, in your account if you're trading on margin or using margin loan privileges.

Trade Execution

Scottrade regularly reviews and assesses market center performance to optimize trade speed and strongly compete against industry averages, helping to ensure orders are executed quickly and efficiently. At the time of this writing, their trade execution speed was 0.10 seconds. This number represents a 6-month rolling average for market orders (100-1999 Shares) in S&P 500 securities.

For more information (like current rates and fees), visit their website: www.scottrade.com/

In Conclusion

For most investors, the strategy is to skip ORD shares. Buy ADRs only and to be patient with the ones that don't trade heavily. Yes, there are fees that can come with acquiring ADRs, but they are small (one to three cents a share annually). In fact, they are often picked up by the issuing company anyway.

Lastly, familiarize yourself with the technical aspects of your broker's trading platform by practicing through a demo account. Each broker has one. Practicing through a demo account is particularly important as this is the same platform you'll be using when you fund your account with real money. It will help you to master the mechanics of entering and exiting trades, not to mention avoid the many mistakes you might make otherwise.

20 Countries Legalizing Cannabis

Overview

The legality of cannabis for general or recreational use varies from country to country. Due to an agreement about Indian hemp, also known as hashish, in the International Opium Convention (1925), possession of cannabis is still illegal in most countries. Currently, Uruguay is the only nation that has completely legalized cannabis for both recreational and medical use.

Recently in the last several years, there's been a wave of optimism as many first world countries have either decriminalized marijuana use, or in some-- like Canada and Australia, full legalization is on its way. There are currently 29 countries that recognize medical marijuana, but only two (Canada and the Netherlands) currently export beyond their borders.

Because legalization is such a new issue, many countries are looking to the United States to see how legalization is working out in states like Colorado, Nevada and Washington. So far, it has been a success. Some of the social and economic benefits include tax revenue increases and decreases in drug-related crime. Countries that have either decriminalized or legalized cannabis have seen positive results across the board, including lower traffic fatalities and opioid abuse, and even nerve cell protection.

In fact, few people know that the US government owns the original patent on Cannabinoids (Cannabis extracts) and lists them as "Neural Protectants" meaning they protect and repair nerves in the brain and body. (worldhealth.net)

The Countries

Starting with North America, below is a list of some of the countries in which the legalization of cannabis is on its way. With cannabis being such a burgeoning industry, the sooner you start your investments, the sooner you can ride the wave to enormous profits. However, countries that have had legal cannabis use for years have been left out, because investment opportunities don't have as much upside. This includes Uruguay, Costa Rica, Netherlands and Spain.

1. United States

This past November, marijuana had a huge victory in the polls. Voters in California, Massachusetts, Maine and Nevada approved recreational marijuana initiatives. On the medical side, voters in Florida, North Dakota and Arkansas passed medical marijuana provisions. Voters in Montana also rolled back restrictions on an existing medical pot law. It was the biggest electoral victory for marijuana reform since 2012, when Colorado and Washington first approved the drug's recreational use.

Federal Legalization

However, medical and recreation use is still illegal on a federal level. Cannabis is still considered a Schedule 1 drug, meaning that the U.S. Drug Enforcement Administration sees no medicinal properties in the substance and classifies it as highly addictive on par with LSD. Therefore, marijuana companies cannot even open a checking account or obtain a line of credit with banks because they're selling a federally illegal substance. If a bank did open an account or a line of credit for a company selling marijuana-related products, it could be construed as money laundering and expose them to substantial fines. In addition, "Marijuana businesses are severely hampered by U.S. Tax Code 280E, which disallows businesses that sell a federal illicit substance from taking normal business deductions." (The Motley Fool)

While the Obama administration decided not to interfere with state regulation, this current Trump administration, led by a very conservative house and senate, may not be as hands-off. In fact, in a few public speeches, they already alluded to the possibility of enforcing federal laws against the states that have legalized recreational use of marijuana. However, while the Department of Justice can take legal action and enforce the federal Controlled Substances Act, if a state decides it does not want to use its courts and police to arrest and punish marijuana users, there is little the federal government can do to change that without using considerable resources.

Two Bills

The good news is that there has been movement on this issue in Washington. There are currently two bills in congress, which involve the legalization of marijuana on the federal level. One of them was introduced on February 27, by Republican Tom Garret of Virginia. His bill *Ending Federal Marijuana Prohibition Act of 2017* would take cannabis off the federally controlled substances list, making it more equal with alcohol and tobacco. (Fool.com)

Nevertheless, the journey to full legalization in the U.S. will be a long one, which is why it's better to invest in international stocks overseas where country-wide legalization will happen much quicker.

Mostly Penny Stocks

Most marijuana stocks in the U.S., like Terra Tech Corp. and mCig Inc., are penny stocks that are thinly traded over the counter rather than on one of the major exchanges. Many of these penny stocks are great companies. However, they cannot grow as fast when they can't even take out a bank loan.

If low risk is a priority, investors do have the option of investing in companies that support the industry rather than those producing the product directly. A few companies that fit this description include Scotts Miracle-Gro (NYSE: SMG) and GW Pharmaceuticals (NASDAQ:GWPH). Though it only makes up 10% of their revenue, Scotts Miracle-Gro acquired multiple hydroponics companies that serve the marijuana-growing industry. In addition, GW Pharmaceuticals' drug Sativex was produced using a formulated extract of the cannabis sativa plant. They sell it in 16 countries outside the United States to treat spasticity associated with multiple sclerosis.

States where Marijuana is Legal

In the United States, the use of cannabis for medical purposes is legal in 28 states, plus the territories of Guam and Puerto Rico, and the District of Columbia, as of November 2017. These states include Alaska, Arizona, Arkansas, California, Colorado, Connecticut, Delaware, Florida, Hawaii, Illinois, Maine, Maryland, Massachusetts, Michigan, Minnesota, Montana, Nevada, New Hampshire, New Jersey, New Mexico, New York, North Dakota, Ohio, Oregon, Pennsylvania, Rhode Island, Vermont, and Washington.

Of those 28 states, 7 have legal recreational marijuana. These include Alaska, California, Colorado, Oregon, Massachusetts, Nevada and Washington. Michigan, Missouri, Vermont, Delaware, and Rhode Island are most likely to be the next states to legalize recreational cannabis. (wikipedia.org)

2. Canada

The Canadian cannabis industry has continued to be a bright light for cannabis investors. Currently, Canada is the exporting hub for companies across the globe to obtain medical cannabis for use by patients in their respective countries. Canada currently exports medical cannabis to Australia, Brazil, Chile, Croatia, Germany, Jamaica and New Zealand.

Marijuana is so in demand right now, that supply in Canada is a real problem. With a completely legal market, licensed producers will reap major profits. Throughout 2016 and 2017, stocks of the cannabis industry were super-hot, and that's before July 2018-- the proposed date in which Canada becomes the first G7 nation to legalize recreational marijuana and unveil its new legislation.

In May 2017, a press release from Health Canada announced that the number of eligible enrollees in Canada's medical-weed program was growing by 10% *a month*!

Legalization

Canadians are overwhelmingly supporting legalized marijuana and the progressive Justin Trudeau administration listened. The administration is currently working on a plan that will work legalized cannabis into the system in an effort to crush black markets, increase tax revenue and create jobs. In the process, Canada will likely end up as the global leader of this emerging commodity.

In December of 2016, the government took a major step by forming a federal task force. This committee released its recommendations relating to the legalization of recreational marijuana and it was very positive. Demand will continue to explode, but it will take time for the program to be up and running. This is why, as we'll learn later, licensed producers have raised plenty of capital from investors who see the big picture. Companies like Canopy Growth (TSE:WEED) and Aphria Inc. (TSE: APH) have been aggressively expanding to increase production capacity. (seekingalpha.com)

Licensed Producers

Analysts believe there will likely be a shortage of cannabis upon legalization because of the difficulty of becoming a licensed producer. Health Canada has approved not much more than 2 percent of applications thus far. Afterwards, in order to legally cultivate and sell cannabis in Canada, each company must be granted a license from Health Canada under the MMPR (Medical Purposes Regulations).

As of now (November 2017), there are 67 cannabis producers that are licensed under the MMPR. The LTB Licensed Producer Composite Index represents the most notable of these LPs, including: Aphria Inc. (OTCQB:APHQF), Aurora Cannabis (OTCQB:ACBFF), Canopy Growth (OTCPK:TWMJF), Emblem Corp. (OTCPK: EMMBF), Emerald Health (OTC:TBQBF), Mettrum Health (OTC:MQTRF), Organigram Holdings, PharmaCan Capital (OTC:PRMCF), Supreme Pharmaceuticals (OTCPK:SPRWF) and THC Biomed Int'l (OTCQB:THCBF).

Risks of Companies Investing in the U.S.

Note on October 2017, the Canadian Securities Administrators set out "specific disclosure expectations" for cannabis companies with investments in the U.S. The staff notice informed that these companies must tell investors about certain risks when they invest in the U.S., due to the prevalent laws against cannabis on the federal level. This includes the potential fallout if the legal landscape for cannabis changes. With this notice, operators of the Toronto Stock Exchange said it may also move to delist stocks of marijuana companies with operations in the United States. These "guidelines apply to all companies with U.S. marijuana-related activities, including direct and indirect involvement in growing and distribution, as well as those that provide goods and services to third parties involved in the U.S. industry." (cbc.ca/news)

Smartly, nearly all the Canadian companies listed in this book sell their marijuana products to countries all over the world (Germany, Mexico, South America, etc.)-- not just the U.S.

Major Canadian licensed producer, Aphria Inc. released a statement responding to both the CSA staff notice and the TSX guidance on October 17. "We believe the new CSA staff notice provides a very balanced framework for the Canadian capital markets," said CEO Vic Neufeld. "We welcome the additional guidance on specific and enhanced disclosure requirements for U.S. marijuana-related activities as they pertain to the medical marijuana industry in Canada." (fool.ca) Recently, Aphria said it was pleased that TSX representatives responded positively to its proactive efforts to work with the Exchange in light of this recent guidance.

Canada's Proposed Pricing and Tax?

As investors and potential customers await Canada's new legislation later in 2018, the biggest concern is taxation. After all, if legalized cannabis is too expensive, customers may turn to the black market. That shouldn't be an option considering Trudeau's goal is to eliminate the black market entirely.

On October 15, 2017, Canadian officials released its tax proposal and it's a big win for licensed producers. For marijuana sales costing up to $10 a gram (or $8 U.S.), there will be a $1-per-gram tax ($0.80 in U.S. currency). Above $10 a gram would be a flat 10%. This outline allows legal marijuana to be priced at a similar level to that of black-market marijuana. In fact, these taxes are a lower rate than alcohol in Canada. (fool.com)

3. Australia

In February of 2016, the Federal Government legalized the growing of cannabis for medicinal and scientific purposes at a federal level. Afterward, the use of medicinal cannabis was legalized by the Victorian government in April 2016, and in New South Wales in August 2016, the usage of medicinal cannabis became legal at the federal level on 1 November 2016, with implementation varying from state-to-state.

Supply and Demand Issue

While not as far in the process as Canada, Australia is increasingly pro-medical marijuana. So much so, there is a big supply and demand problem. The government has indicated it's open to speeding things up, with Health Minister Greg Hunt recently announcing that authorities will allow more rapid importation of the commodity while a domestic supply is built. (theguardian.com)

Canopy Growth to the Rescue

To counter delays for patients who have been prescribed medical cannabis, importers will now be allowed to buy from established suppliers overseas, then store it locally to be distributed via doctors. Mega Canadian weed producer, Canopy Growth Corporation (TSE: WEED) has this relationship with Australian company AusCann Group Holdings (ASX: AC8). According to AusCann Managing Director Elaine Darby, the agreement will cement AusCann's leadership position in Australia's rapidly developing medicinal cannabis market. You can read more about Canopy Growth's rapid ascension and market dominance in the next chapter. (newcannabisventures.com)

Bill to Make Cannabis More Accessible for Terminally-Ill Passes Senate

A bill by the Australian Greens to give terminally-ill patients quicker, easier access to doctor-prescribed medicinal cannabis, passed the upper house on October 19, 2017. It will now go before the lower house, where the government controls the numbers. During the debate, Liberal Democrat Senator Leyonhjelm said the Turnbull Government had "blood on its hands" for not making access easier. "They are responsible for terrible unnecessary suffering and very likely a number of premature deaths," he said. (news.com.au/)

4. Brazil

Recreational Cannabis in Brazil is still technically illegal, but possession and cultivation of personal amounts were decriminalized in 2006 and in 2017. Limited cannabis-based medicines are now permitted. In January, Brazil issued its first license for a cannabis-based medicine, allowing sales of an oral spray called Sativex by GW Pharmaceuticals.

Bedrocan Brazil

Canopy Growth Corp., which owns Bedrocan, has teamed up with Brazilian company Entourage Phytolab SA and founded a new subsidiary, Bedrocan Brazil. The latter imports products from Canopy Growth Corp. (TSE:WEED), while Entourage Phytolab SA will develop more medical cannabis products. (insiderfinancial.com)

When the market matures in South America, Bedrocan Brazil plans to produce and cultivate its own cannabis. But for now, it will begin by importing from its Canadian parent company, Canopy Growth.

HempMeds Brasil

On October 9, 2017 Medical Marijuana Inc (OTCMKTS:MJNA) reported that its subsidiary HempMeds Brasil will support the launch of the Associação Nacional dos usuários de Canabidiol Patient Association in Brazil. This association is "committed to connecting people with cannabis-friendly physicians and continuing to update on the Brazilian medical community and its members on the therapeutic applications of cannabis." (mmjreporter.com)

5. Chile

In 2005, Chile formally decriminalized all cannabis use. Since 2014, Chile has allowed the cultivation of cannabis for medical purposes with the authorization of The Chilean Agriculture Service (SAG).

More recently in 2016, a regulation bill was passed that now allows Chileans to grow small amounts of marijuana for medical, recreational or spiritual use. It was approved by the country's lower house of Congress.

Fundación Daya

AusCann (ASX: AC8) has entered into an agreement to form a joint-venture with Chilean group Fundación Daya-- the only group so far to have a medical cannabis production license in Chile. (seekingalpha.com)

Chile's Neighbor Peru Also Legalizing

In late 2017, lawmakers in Peru have voted overwhelmingly in favor of a bill to legalize medical marijuana, allowing cannabis oil to be locally produced, imported and sold. The medicinal use of cannabis is now legal in Peru, Colombia and Chile. In Uruguay, marijuana cultivation and use is permitted in all its forms.

6. Columbia

Since 1994, cannabis has been legalized for possession of small amounts up to 22 grams for personal consumption. However, in 2016, the Supreme Court of Justice stated that someone who is caught with a greater amount than the statutory limit cannot be criminally prosecuted if it is found that the person carries the substance to satisfy their own consumption needs.

A Canadian company called PharmaCielo, with the government's approval, is working to produce the drug legally in Colombia. The government has begun processing licenses for a small number of companies, including PharmaCielo, under a 2015 law that allows the cultivation of medical marijuana. (nytimes.com)

7. Czech Republic

Since 2010, possession of up to fifteen grams of cannabis for personal use or cultivation of up to five plants is a misdemeanor subject to minor fine. However, this is mostly not enforced. Medical use of cannabis on prescription has been legal and regulated since 2013. (wikipedia.org)

The Czech Republic has become a huge tourist attraction for marijuana enthusiasts, especially in Prague. As more and more countries begin to legalize recreational pot, they'll certainly do so as well to continue bringing in those tourists.

An Australian exchange listed cannabis company called MGC Pharmaceuticals is developing a library of medicinal cannabis research with the Royal Institute of Melbourne. They have a 5-year research partnership with Panax Pharma in the Czech Republic.

8. Ecuador

Production and distribution of cannabis in Ecuador is still prohibited. However, a movement is brewing as more and more public authorities are in favor of the non-criminalization of drug use in small doses. Ecuador is looking very closely to Uruguay, its neighboring country where it has regularized the marijuana market for years. It is not illegal to carry up to ten grams of cannabis in Ecuador. Despite the laws, police barely enforce them. (wikipedia.org)

Marijuana plants grow regularly in Ecuador due to its perfect climate for cultivation. The city of Cuenca in Ecuador is even known for their cannabis-infused chocolate, which give consumers a "mellow vibration." (Cuencahighlife.com)

9. Germany

Germany is a cannabis-friendly country with a quarter of the population having consumed cannabis. That's almost 19 million people. Medical use became legal in 2017, along with a federal mandate for cheap access. German Health Minister, Hermann Gröhe, presented the legal draft on the legalization of medical cannabis to the cabinet, which took effect early in the year.

For Ill Patients Only

The Cabinet of Germany approved the measure for legal medical cannabis for seriously ill patients who have consulted with a doctor and "have no therapeutic alternative". That means that public health insurance companies, which cover 90% of Germans, are on the front line of the cannabis efficacy issue. Consequently, Germany's medical market is potentially one of the most lucrative cannabis markets in the world, perhaps even rivaling California's recreational market. (CNN)

Recreational marijuana is still technically illegal in Germany, though laws are not enforced against people who are caught possessing less than 15 grams. Very similar to the United States, the law on marijuana consumption is decided in each of Germany's 16 federal states.

Imported Marijuana

Germany is EU's most populous state with 82 million people. Yet at this time, it will rely entirely on imported marijuana for its patients. Canopy Growth Corporation (TSE:WEED) announced in November 2017 that it had entered into an agreement to acquire MedCann GmbH Pharma and Nutraceuticals (MedCann), a private pharmaceutical distributor in Germany. MedCann has already successfully placed Canopy Growth branded products in German pharmacies. Led by Dr. Pierre Debs, MedCann's team has established itself as a leading cannabis importer and distributor within Germany. (newcannabisventures.com)

Canadian LP, Aurora Cannabis Inc has become a top contender for cultivation in Germany, and has "quietly issued an ex-im license by both Canadian and German authorities. Publicly, this has been described as an effort to help stem the now chronic cannabis shortage facing patients who attempt to go through legitimate, prescribed channels. On the German side, intriguingly, this appears to be a provisional license." (cannabisindustryjournal.com)

German Medical Cannabis Crops?

At present, the German bid process is several months behind schedule. Germany's path to officially grow its own medical cannabis crops has not been a smooth one. In April 2017, the government released its bid at the ICBC conference, which held its first annual gathering in Berlin. The requirements of the bid was for a small amount of cannabis (2,000 kg), with "mandated experience producing high qualities of medical marijuana in a federally legitimate market. By definition that excluded all German hopefuls, and set up Canada and Holland as the only countries who could provide such experience, capital and backlog of crop as the growing gets started." (cannabisindustryjournal.com)

10. Argentina

Argentina is another country on the growing list of Latin countries to recently legalize medical marijuana. In fact, medical marijuana comes with no cost to patients.

This was made possible by a group of 136 Argentine families who petitioned their government to allow marijuana use to treat their children who suffered from epilepsy, autism, and other ailments. As you'll see, this is much like Mexico's story. (Drugpolicy.org)

11. Israel

On March 5, 2017, Israel's Cabinet decriminalized the recreational use of marijuana, at its weekly meeting on Sunday in a move applauded by politicians from across the spectrum, left to right. The policy decriminalizes the illegal use of cannabis. However, growing and selling the plant would remain illegal. Not long after, 37 farmers received preliminary permits from the Health Ministry to construct facilities for the plant's cultivation. They will join an existing group of 8 medical-cannabis growers in the country.

Justice Minister Ayelet Shaked said in a statement, "Israel cannot shut its eyes to the changes being made across the world in respect to marijuana consumption and its effects." (CNN)

Leading the Way in Research

Already a worldwide leader on marijuana-related research funded by the government, Israel's government has allowed medical marijuana as a tonic for intractable illnesses since 1992. Home to Raphael Mechoulam, the pioneer of marijuana research, Israel is where THC and the endocannabinoid system were first discovered. It has also become somewhat of a safe haven for American cannabis companies seeking to overcome federal roadblocks. In fact, one can argue that medical marijuana now being legal in 29 U.S. states and counting, is a direct result of Israeli research, which has in many way ways legitimized the study of cannabis.

Lack of Supply

With pot legalization spreading like wildfire across globally, Israel believes marijuana can be a huge export for them. However, until Israel can ship medical marijuana to other countries within a few years, their biggest problem at the moment is a lack of supply. Consequently, Israel has lessened restrictions to allow more production facilities to grow and process weed.

The Israeli government has approved the export of medicinal marijuana products, enabling companies there to gain a sizable piece of the U.S. market. While importing cannabis into the United States is still federally illegal, companies can get around that ban by receiving drug approval from the FDA (Federal Drug Administration). According to the FDA, nothing is stopping them, as long as they meet the agency's strict requirements for approval.

"According to Saul Kaye, the founder of iCAN, an Israeli cannabis R&D firm, 2016 saw the investment of more than $250 million in Israeli cannabis companies and startups – half of that investment came from North America. Kaye predicts that investment will grow ten-fold over the next two years, reaching $1 billion. At least 50 American cannabis companies – and counting – have established R&D operations in Israel." (rollingstone.com)

Listed within the next chapter are 2 Israel-based publicly traded companies with plenty of potential. These companies are Teva Pharmaceuticals Industries (NYSE: TEVA) and One World Cannabis Ltd. (OTC: OWCP).

12. Jamaica

Jamaica is in the early stages of setting up a medical cannabis industry. In early January 2017, the Cannabis Licensing Authority granted conditional approval to three applicants for permits to cultivate and process marijuana. This comes almost a year after the passing of regulations to facilitate the cultivation of marijuana for medicinal, scientific, and therapeutic purposes.

On October 19, 2017, "Jamaica's Cannabis Licensing Authority has granted its first approvals for the nation's medical cannabis industry, as Everything Oily Labs Limited was issued a processing license and Epican was issued a license to cultivate," the Jamaica Gleaner reports.

Hyacinth Lightborne, chair of the CLA, indicated that 3 other applications were also approved, another 57 applicants are 'in the conditional approval stage,' and lastly, 209 other applications 'are currently being processed.' (ganjapreneur.com)

Canopy Growth Corp Again

On October 25, Canopy Growth Corp. signed a deal to form a strategic partnership in Jamaica. The Canadian marijuana company says Jamaican company, Grow House JA Ltd. will now operate as Tweed Ltd JA. and serve the Jamaican medical cannabis market.

13. Mexico

On December 13, 2016, Mexico's senate voted to legalize medical marijuana, seeing potential for CBD. Earlier that year, patients in dire need were granted permits by the pressured Mexican Health Department to receive hemp-based CBD oil from overseas--specifically a California-based company called HempMeds, a subsidiary of Medical Marijuana Inc (OTC: MJNA). This came after years of medical marijuana advocates pleaded on behalf of two Mexican families with children suffering from severe epilepsy.

"We, Mexicans know all too well the range and the defects of prohibitionist and punitive policies, and of the so-called war on drugs that has prevailed for 40 years," President Enrique Pena Nieto said. "Our country has suffered, as few have the ill effects of organized crime tied to drug trafficking. Fortunately, a new consensus is gradually emerging worldwide in favor of reforming drug policies. A growing number of countries are strenuously combating criminals, but instead of criminalizing consumers, they offer them alternatives and opportunities."

Bill Finally Signed by Pena Nieto

In May 2017, the lower house of Mexico's Congress overwhelmingly passed the bill. Then on June 19, Mexican President Enrique Pena Nieto finally signed the bill into law.

The bill aims to classify the psychoactive component of cannabis tetrahydrocannabinol (THC) as a "therapeutic." Legalization of medical cannabis in Mexico would give pot-based businesses yet another avenue to legally sell their product beyond Canada and the

United States. HempMeds continues its partnership with the Mexican Health Department. For most of 2017, it sold the only legal cannabis-based products allowed into Mexico.

According to Stuart Titus, the CEO of Medical Marijuana, Inc., legalizing medical marijuana in Mexico represents a "$1 billion to $2 billion opportunity" in cumulative revenue over the next decade, according to an interview with Fortune.

14. New Zealand

After alcohol and tobacco, marijuana is already the third most widely used recreational drug in New Zealand, and the most widely used illegal drug. According to the World Drug Report, this ranks as the ninth highest cannabis consumption level in the world. The use of marijuana in New Zealand is governed by the Misuse of Drugs Act 1975, which makes unauthorized possession of any amount of cannabis illegal.

In March 2016, New Zealand's Associate Health Minister Peter Dunne stated he would back policy changes regarding medical marijuana if it is proven to be effective in treating illnesses.

Marijuana Referendum

After nine years of conservative rule, liberal Jacinda Ardern was confirmed as the nation's next prime minister on October 19, 2017. Ardern promptly announced she would hold a referendum on whether to legalize recreational marijuana at some point over the next 3 years. She did not mention if she personally favored legalization.

"I've always been very open about the fact that I do not believe that people should be imprisoned for personal use of cannabis," Ardern said. "On the flip side, I also have concerns around young people accessing a product which can clearly do harm and damage to them." (washingtonpost.com)

15. Portugal

In 2001, Portugal became the first country ever to decriminalize the use of all drugs– making possession of personal quantities of all drugs, including cannabis, a non-criminal offence. Since then, Portugal has experienced major benefits, including a decrease in "hard" drug use and drug related crimes. (forbes.com)

However, in 2003, an amendment was made that criminalized the sale and possession of any cannabis seed not certified as of a European hemp variety. This mostly means Portugal is largely opposed to cultivation, even banning the sale of equipment intended for cultivation. Furthermore, Portugal's neighboring country of Spain has such a well-developed cannabis market that many users in Portugal rely on cannabis grown in Spain or imported from Morocco. This is especially true in the case of hashish.

In 2017, Portugal continually decriminalized possession of marijuana by softening up its laws. So much so, that in September, Canadian marijuana producers finally acquired a license from the Portuguese government to import cannabis seeds and clones. This is a major win for Canadian investors, as it will open up a whole new market in Europe. Tilray CEO Brendan Kennedy said that given its warm weather, "Portugal seemed like the ideal location to grow plants." (greencamp.com)

16. Puerto Rico

In 2015 the Governor of Puerto Rico signed an executive order to legalize cannabis for medicinal use only.

Governor Garcia-Padilla said in a statement to the press: "We're taking a significant step in the area of health that is crucial to our development and high expectations for their quality of life. I am sure that many patients will receive appropriate treatment that will offer them new hope." (fortaleza.pr.gov)

Government Learning Curve Issues?

In 2017, medical marijuana dispensaries in Puerto Rico began operating for the first time in the U.S. territory. However, the Puerto Rican government has not made the process easy for everyone. Patients, tourists, and business owners are all having trouble operating within the current system. There are over 11,000 patients in Puerto Rico awaiting their patient ID cards. There just isn't enough employees processing applications and not enough places for patients to submit and receive their paperwork. (hightimes.com)

17. South Africa

Early in 2017, medical marijuana, known as dagga to South Africans, was approved by the country's government. Dr. Mario Oriani-Ambrosini created the Medical Innovation Bill in 2014, which proposed the complete legalization of medical and recreational cannabis. After being diagnosed with stage IV lung cancer, Dr. Oriani-Ambrosini became a major advocate for the legalization of cannabis before his death in August 2014. (merryjane.com)

Regulation on the Way

The Medical Control Council, South Africa's medical regulatory agency that uses a variety of experts to evaluate the distribution and marketing of medicine, is in the process of forming new guidelines for the production of cannabis oil and other cannabis products.

Recently, the ban on using cannabis recreationally is being challenged in the High Court, raising the possibility that it could effectively be decriminalized some time in 2018. (mg.co.za)

18. Poland

On July 24, 2017, Poland's Lower House of Parliament overwhelmingly voted to legalize medical marijuana. A recommendation from the nation's Health Care Committee helped enormously. The bill was authored by MP Piotr Liroy-Marzec, who has long been an advocate for the legalization of medical cannabis. Liroy-Marzec's original proposal would have allowed Polish citizens to cultivate their own medical cannabis. However, Polish legislators dropped that provision, instead opting in favor of a regulatory system. Therefore, Polish patients will rely on a limited number of medical cannabis exporters, most likely from licensed producers in Canada. (newcannabisventures.com)

In November 2017, it became official that imported plants can now be used to make prescription drugs in Polish pharmacies. Radio Poland states the bill comes into effect next October. It will allow medical marijuana to be prescribed in many forms, including tinctures and resin.

The Polish Pharmaceutical Chamber estimates that "up to 300,000 patients" could qualify for medical marijuana. "The law is unrestrictive, giving doctors leeway to prescribe marijuana to any medical condition if its usefulness is supported by research." (konbini.com)

19. Italy

Marijuana for medical or religious purposes is legal here, but still illegal if used for recreational purposes. The country first legalized medical marijuana in 2007.

Getting caught with even small amounts of marijuana for personal use can still land you a misdemeanor. However, Liberties.eu reports that it's more likely you will just pay a fine, especially if you are a first time offender.

Cannabis businesses have been so successful that growers have actually complained about not being able to keep up with demand. Earlier this year, several political groups began a movement to legalize recreational marijuana. They've collected over 68,000 signatures, but the national government has not yet discussed a proposal. (forbes.com)

20. Greece

In July 2017, Greece announced a new law permitting the use of medical marijuana. Prime Minister Alexis Tsipras stated that medical professionals in Greece will soon be able to prescribe cannabis for various medical conditions.

Health Minister Andreas Xanthos announced in May that medical cannabis preparations could be manufactured and packaged soon, although the exact guidelines for this process are still to be determined. If deemed necessary, production, packaging, and marketing for Greece will be developed by the state, Xanthos emphasized. (marijuana.com)

The 20 Best Globally Traded Marijuana Companies

Overview

For reasons this book illustrated earlier, most of the best publicly traded pot companies do not reside in the United States where much uncertainty still prevails. You will find the bulk of the fastest growing marijuana companies are listed in the exchanges of foreign countries, like Canada and Australia. This is why this chapter primarily lists foreign stocks. With the help of the brokers listed previously in this book, investors will find that it's just as easy to get a piece of the pot action in these foreign countries as it is in your own country.

As a reminder, with top brokerages like Interactive Brokers, shares in these companies can be bought in the American over-the-counter (OTC) markets or directly from its original exchange. This is why each listed stock below will have ticker symbols listed for 2 markets-- its native exchange and its version on the OTC market. For instance, Canopy Growth Corporation has the ticker WEED on the TSE exchange. However, on the OTC market, its ticker is TWMJF. With either one, you are at the mercy of the prevailing currency rate, so do your due diligence before trading.

The companies on the next page were listed based on data analysis, market share, strong leadership and trending prices that have led to dozens of triple-digit profits over the past few years. And make no mistake, there will be plenty more companies coming in 2018. Lastly, remember that past performance is no guarantee of success.

Without further delay, here's the definitive list of the best, safest, fastest growing companies in the pot biz.

The Stocks

1. Aphria Inc. (OTCQB:APHQF, TSE:APH)

Aphria, Inc. is maybe the top Canadian licensed producer engaging in the production and supply of medical marijuana. At the time of this writing, its share price over the last 12 months had soared upwards of 500% to a market cap in excess of $1 billion. Along with other top licensed producers in Canada, Aphria outperformed 94% of TSE-listed stocks in the same period. The company was founded by Cole Cacciavillani and John Cervini on June 22, 2011 and is headquartered in Leamington, Canada.

Aphria is a company that often gets overlooked by investors searching for the ultimate marijuana stock. For the reasons outlined below, it might be a better long-term buy than the larger, more popular Canopy Growth Corporation.

Revenue

Aphria delivered incredible fiscal Q1'18 results, that included high revenues, higher gross profit, increases in kilograms sold, improvements in product cost, resulting in huge % gains in its stock's price.

Year over year, Aphria's revenues increased 39.8% to $6.12 million. Adjusted gross profits increased 43% to $4.77 million. The most impressive stat is Aphria's increasingly lower production costs. The company's costs in cash to produce a gram of dried cannabis decreased 14.4% from the 4th quarter to $0.95 per gram. No other Canadian LP is heading in the right direction like Aphria. It currently enjoys the lowest production costs among the LPs of Canada. If Aphria can continue to minimize costs and achieve larger margins, they can distance themselves from the competition in the long run.

While revenues improved 39.8% year over year, the costs of that production increased a 27.7% to $1.35 million. That's an excellent ratio. The deviance between revenue growth and production costs allowed Aphria to drive gross profits before fair value adjustments up 43.7% to $4.77 million. After adjustments, gross profits for the quarter were $7.9 million.

Aphria's expenses more than doubled to $6.52 million. However, this expenditure is necessary as they aggressively expand in preparation of Canada's legalization. Aphria still improved net income by nearly 1600% year over year. All of this resulted in earnings of $0.11 a share versus $0.01 a year ago. (fool.com)

Expansion

It's through its expansionary projects to increase scale that has allowed Aphria to continually drive down its cash costs to produce. With its ongoing expansion, continued large revenue growth can be expected. Aphria just completed a 1,000,000-square-foot cannabis cultivation facility that should increase output to 70,000 kg of dried cannabis every year. Financed by an equity offering, this includes 700,000 square feet of automated greenhouses, 230,000 square feet of infrastructure including vaults, processing and warehouse areas.

The increased production capacity not only improves their production costs, but also gives Aphria the opportunity to be ahead of the game in terms of supply. Many investors worry that Canada will struggle to produce the quantity needed for a recreational consumer base. This aggressive expansion by Aphria is great news to shareholders.

The expansion is expected to finish in 2018, and should set up Aphria perfectly for the pending Canadian legalization of cannabis for recreational use.

Investments

Aphria has a large portion of its investments in the North American cannabis industry mostly through its stake in Liberty Health Services. Aphria's investments include companies Canabo Medical, CannaRoyalty, Copperstate Farms, Green Acre Capital, Kalytera Therapeutics, MassRoots, Resolve Digital Health and Scythian BioSciences.

Aphria also provides consultative services to Nuuvera in return for a piece of the company's sales. Their deal is estimated to be at least $10 million a year once production is achieved; which should drive Aphria's net profits even higher. (aphria.com)

Conclusion

Aphria's management has smartly scaled the company with the growth of the industry, as opposed to building too fast. With recreational cannabis being fully legalized with completed legislation in 2018, Aphria has put itself in an advantageous position, ensuring it will be a market leader in the Canadian cannabis market for years to come.

Visit www.aphria.com/ for more current information.

Company Highlights

Market Capitalization: $841.8 M

Shares Outstanding: 138.9 M

Price/ Earnings: 50.32

Revenue: $15.4 M

Net Profit Margin: 84.60%

Return on Equity: 8.46%

Industry: Pharmaceuticals

Share Price 52 Week Range: $2.55- 6.60

Company Profile

Address: 269 Erie Street West, Leamington, Ontario N8H 3C4

Phone: +1.844.427.4742

Number of Employees: 150

Chairman, President & Chief Executive Officer: Victor Neufeld

Chief Operating Officer & Director: Cole Cacciavillani

Chief Financial Officer: Carl A. Merton

Chief Scientific Officer: Gary Leong

2. Canopy Growth Corporation (TSE:WEED) (OTCQB:TWMJF)

Founded by Bruce Linton on August 5, 2009 and headquartered in Smith Falls, Canada. Canopy Growth Corporation supplies an unmatched selection of premium medical marijuana, with exposure to ever-growing markets in Canada, U.S., Germany, Denmark, Australia, Jamaica and South America.

Incredible Growth

The company has recorded strong growth on pretty much all metrics and at the end of 2017, Canopy Growth reported to have over 58,000 registered patients which is more than 260% higher than the previous year. After Trudeau announced his goal to legalize the recreational market in Canada in 2017, Canopy Growth's stock price hit amazing highs of $14.39 U.S. dollars, becoming the first publicly traded pot stock to have a market cap over $1 billion.

Last year, Canopy Growth emerged as one of the most dominant medical marijuana suppliers in the world. It also ingeniously changed its TSX ticker to WEED and announced its acquisition of Mettrum Health Corp. which gives it plenty of leverage to capitalize on recreational use in Canada and eventually the United States. (nasdaq.com)

Revenue

Canopy's 2018 first quarter earnings report featured numerous highlights. Revenue was $15.9 million, a 127% increase over the three month period that ended June 30, 2016 when revenue totaled

$7.0, and an 8% increase over fourth quarter of fiscal 2017 revenues of $14.7 million.

Some revenue was understandably lost as Canopy subsidiaries Mettrum, Tweed and Bedrocan were mostly made inactive through the latter half of the fourth quarter fiscal 2017 and the first quarter fiscal 2018. This was because they were integrated with new standard quality control procedures, as well as being launched into the Tweed Main Street online store.

CEO Bruce Linton, "Recording sales of $1M in a single day earlier this year revealed many points in our sales, fulfillment and shipping infrastructure that needed strengthening. With many customers asking to be able to access all products under the canopy, it made perfect sense for us to transition, in April, from multiple, single brand sites to the Tweed Main Street marketplace. Bringing all products of our many leading brands together under one roof, to provide a shopping experience similar to what customers expect in many other markets, has strengthened our leadership position."

Canopy Growth also sold 1,830 kilograms and kilogram equivalents. This is an 86% increase over first quarter fiscal 2017. They harvested 5,575 kg, mostly attributed to the Tweed Farms greenhouse harvest. This is compared to 1,882 kg during the same period last year, which represents an 196% increase over first quarter fiscal 2017. This weighted average cost per gram of cultivation to harvest and post-harvest costs was $1.28 per gram, compared to $1.64 per gram in the first quarter of last year and to $1.46 per gram in the fourth quarter of last year, which shows excellent promise. (prnewswire.com).

Since 2014, the revenue has grown about 5000% making it the fastest growing LP in Canada. The revenue for Canopy is expected to increase at a rate of about 200% annually and the earnings at a rate of 142% quarterly. No wonder it is the first billion dollar Marijuana stock.

Expansion

Through its aggressive expansion, Canopy is expected to produce 100,000kgs of product by mid-2018. Canopy Growth recently announced plans to develop up to three million square feet of greenhouse growing capacity in British Columbia. This facility will help Canopy significantly scale up the production footprint. (smallcappower.com)

Besides the companies mentioned above, Canopy Growth also acquired German marijuana distributor MedCann, giving it a major distribution network in Europe. This will ultimately put Canopy Growth (Tweed-branded) cannabis strains into pharmacies in Germany, where medical marijuana has been legal since 2005. With a highly experienced leadership team, led by Dr. Pierre Debs, MedCann has established itself as a leading marijuana importer and distributor within Germany where the cannabis industry still relies solely on imports.

In addition, Canopy Growth announced an export deal with Brazil. Their wholly owned subsidiary, Bedrocan Canada Inc., completed their first ever export of dried cannabis from Canada to Brazil. Canopy hopes to work towards building a solidified medicinal cannabis platform in Brazil. (seekingalpha.com)

As mentioned in the last section, Canopy Growth Corp. also signed a deal to form a strategic partnership in Jamaica. The Canadian marijuana company says Jamaican company, Grow House JA Ltd. (in which Canopy has a 49% stake) will now operate as Tweed Ltd JA. and serve the Jamaican medical cannabis market. Tweed JA has conditional license approvals and has begun construction of its facility. (bnn.ca)

Investments

Like Aphria, Canopy is also doing its fair share of investing and marketing. With its acquisition of Mettrum, Canopy has brought its production capacity to 665,000 square feet. Its marketing efforts include a partnership with famously pro-pot supporter and musician Snoop Dog.

Canopy also launched the sale of Canada's first encapsulated cannabis oil soft gels on June 19, 2017. Industrial cannabis oil extraction system is now operational.

Lastly, Canopy has $115.5 million in cash and cash equivalents at quarter end.

Fortune 500 Company Stake

Constellation Brands, Inc., a Fortune 500 company that owns brands such as Corona beer, Black Velvet Whisky and Casa Noble tequila recently agreed to take a 9.9% stake in Canopy Growth Corporation. The two companies plan to work together to develop and market beverages that will be infused with Cannabis. (wsj.com)

Conclusion

In order to justify Canopy Growth Corporation's amazing ascent and acquire new investors, management will need to boost sales enough to offset its costly expansion projects. However, keep in mind, a company at its stage of development should be spending on future growth anyway. Not giving back to shareholders. Nevertheless,

Canopy Growth is establishing a worldwide presence amid a shift toward greater acceptance of marijuana use.

Visit canopygrowth.com for more current information.

Company Highlights

Market Capitalization: $1.7 B

Shares Outstanding: 171.3 M

Revenue: $30.4 M

Industry: Agricultural Commodities/ Milling

Share Price 52 Week Range: $4.15- 14.39

Company Profile

Address: 1 Hershey Drive, Smith Falls, Ontario K7A 0A8

Phone: +1.855.558.9333

Number of Employees: 546

Chairman: Bruce Linton

Chief Operating Officer & Director: Cole Cacciavillani

Chief Financial Officer & Senior Vice President: Timothy R. Saunders

Managing Director: Mark Zekulin

3. Aurora Cannabis Inc. (ACB:TSXV) (OTCQB: ACBFF)

Another licensed producer with a market cap in excess of $1 billion, Aurora Cannabis Inc. is headquartered in Vancouver, Canada. Its medical cannabis products include Borealis Blend, Odin, Odin 3, Peechee, Sentinel, Stokes, and Warwick 2. Aurora's product types include Tetrahydrocannabinol (THC), Cannabidiole (CBD), Indica, Sativa and hybrid.

Canopy Growth Corp. remains ahead of Aurora on our list because it has the advantage of its branding, many export deals and a first-mover position in the market. However, with its strong fundamentals and expansion deals, Aurora may overtake Canopy by the end of 2018.

Revenue

Quarter to quarter, Aurora's revenue recently increased 15% to $5.9M. Year to year, that is a 387% increase. Investors can expect this growth to continue at least over the next few quarters, until the mid-2018 when implemented recreational marijuana legislation causes the growth rate to be significantly higher.

Most cannabis stocks are trading at higher valuations due to the industry's future expectations and enormous potential. Aurora's higher valuation can be justified given its high, double-digit revenue growth rate of 15%. Even though Canopy Growth Corporation generates 2x the revenue compared to Aurora, this difference may narrow as investors focus on margins and the bottom-line. With its low cost production, Aurora could likely end up more attractive than Canopy.

Expansion

As will be mentioned many times in this book, there is currently a lack of supply in the industry. The upcoming Canadian legalization of marijuana in July 2018 for recreational use will further drive demand to the sky. With its low-cost production, Aurora hopes to meet the demands of both the medical and anticipated recreational opportunities. Meeting customer demand has been an issue that many companies in the industry have faced. However, Aurora has been building their inventory since 2016 in an effort to gain market share from competitors like the Canopy and Aurora.

In April 2017, Aurora completed its acquisition of Peloton Pharmaceuticals Inc. Peloton is constructing a 40,000 square foot cannabis production facility in Pointe Claire, Quebec that is nearly complete. (fool.ca)

Also in 2017, Aurora Cannabis secured a nearly 20% stake in Cann Group, a publicly traded Australian company. Cann Group is the first company in Australia to be licensed for the cultivation and research of medicinal cannabis. Its IPO took place in May 2017. With this smart investment, Aurora could find its way into more markets, especially the rapidly developing Australian market. (streetregister.com)

In October 2017, Aurora Cannabis raised an additional $60 million through equity bought deal financings to further its aggressive expansion, as well as to fund its international growth program. Given the significant demand for this bought deal financing, Aurora agreed to raise another $6 million. After this development, Aurora Cannabis will have almost $220 million in cash, which is a significant plus when expansion is a necessity. (smallcappower.com)

Lastly, Aurora recently announced its intention to make a strategic investment in Hempco Food and Fiber Inc. This will provide access to a potential source of low-cost raw CBD material for extraction.

Growing Customer Base

Currently, Canopy Growth produces six times more product than Aurora Cannabis, but future expectations look similar with both companies aiming for 100,000kg by mid-2018.

Aurora has gone from zero to over 20,000 customers in less than two years, 3,500 patients since fiscal year end. At the time of this writing, Aurora controls about 15% of Canada's medical marijuana based on total grams sold. It also has 8% of all customers, though keep in mind patients can get their medical cannabis from multiple producers.

Furthermore, Aurora is providing clients and the general public with access to a simplified Certificate of Analysis (CoA) for every one of the company's cannabis products available for sale. This new protocol will give customers secure knowledge that an independent third-party laboratory had tested Aurora's products for a wide range of potential contaminants.

In September 2017, Aurora announced it had received all the required permits to ship dried cannabis flower from Canada to Germany. This enabled the company to begin supplying the German medical marijuana market through its wholly-owned subsidiary Pedanios GmbH ("Pedanios"), Germany's top medical cannabis distributor. (newswire.ca)

Conclusion

Investors are excitedly investing in this marijuana producer, with the potential to provide enormous returns heading into recreational legalization. With so much cash on the books, aggressive expansion and an ever increasing revenue, Aurora Cannabis Inc. is looking to be Canada's top licensed pot producer. To do so, it will need to ramp up production to meet an expected supply shortfall.

Visit auroramj.com for more current information.

Company Highlights

Market Capitalization: $832.7 M

Shares Outstanding: 375.1 M

Revenue: $13.6 M

Industry: Agriculture/ Milling

Share Price 52 Week Range: $0.31 - 2.96

Company Profile

Address: 1199 West Hastings Street, Vancouver, British Columbia V6E 3T5

Phone: +1.604.669.9788

Number of Employees: 171

Chief Executive Officer & Non-Independent Director: Terry Booth

President & Director: Steve Dobler

Chief Financial Officer: Glen W. Ibbott

Executive Vice President: Cam Battley

4. GW Pharmaceuticals (NASDAQ:GWPH)

Based in the U.K., there's a very good chance that GW Pharmaceuticals could be consistently profitable by 2020 with its endeavors in cannabis-related medicinal products. With a market cap of $2.5 billion, GW Pharmaceuticals is a drug development company that focuses on discovering cannabinoids from the cannabis plant. GW Pharmaceuticals' research is to discover uses of cannabinoids to treat cancer pain, diabetes, schizophrenia, glioma, epilepsy and much more. (fool.com)

Earnings

The company's latest earnings reported ($2.07) EPS for the 3rd quarter of 2017 missed the estimates of many analysts. However, the company had an encouraging boost in revenue of $3.14 million during the quarter, compared to analyst estimates of $2.10 million. "On average, equities analysts anticipate that GW Pharmaceuticals PLC will post ($6.16) earnings per share for the current fiscal year." (nasdaq.com)

The company's lead cannabinoid product is Epidiolex, which is a liquid formulation of pure plant-derived cannabidiol. It currently has negative earnings. Nevertheless, the FDA gave GW Pharmaceuticals a seven-year exclusive right to use Epidiolex for treatment of tuberous sclerosis complex (TSC). TSC is a rare disorder known to cause many cases of epilepsy. The drug has been a success. Patients have reported experiencing 39% fewer seizures than before, confirming for many the effectiveness of cannabinoids.

Other Drugs

The firm also offers Sativex (nabiximols), which has been mostly used for the treatment of spasticity due to multiple sclerosis (MS). At the time of this writing, Sativex is not yet approved for sale in any form in the United States, since it failed an important phase 3 study on cancer pain. Regardless, Sativex has been approved for use in 30 other countries, including New Zealand and many territories in Europe. (forbes.com)

Conclusion

With plenty of cash on hand and nearly no debt, GW Pharmaceuticals is poised to increase investments in more research and development, leading analysts to predict a rise in this marijuana stock's market value.

Visit gwpharm.com for more current information.

Company Highlights

Market Capitalization: $2.5 B

Shares Outstanding: 302.5 M

Revenue: $14.6 M

Industry: Pharmaceuticals

Share Price 52 Week Range: $7.68 - 11.28

Company Profile

Address: Sovereign House, Cambridge, Cambridgeshire CB24 9BZ

Phone: +44.1223.266800

Number of Employees: 496

Chief Executive Officer & Executive Director: Justin D. Gover

Chief Operating Officer & Executive Director: Christopher John Tovey

Chief Financial Officer: Scott M. Giacobello

Director-Clinical Operations: Richard Potts

5. Innovative Industrial Properties Inc. (NYSE: IIPR)

Innovative Industrial Properties Inc. is the first U.S. company to be included on this list. It operates as an open-ended real estate investment trust (REIT).

What is an REIT?

For those of you who do not know, a real estate investment trust is a company that owns and operates, income-producing real estate, ranging from apartment buildings to warehouses, hospitals, shopping centers and hotels. Stockholders of a REIT earn a large share of the income produced through the company's real estate investments. REITs are required to pay at least 90 percent of its taxable income in the form of shareholder dividends each year.

Innovative Industrial Properties is not as established as the other companies on this list, having just been added to NYSE late last year.

On the NYSE

So why is it so high on this list? Besides an actual dividend of 1.55%, the New York Stock Exchange made a rare move and allowed Industrial Properties to be included on their exchange. This is despite marijuana's illegal status on the federal level in the U.S. Therefore, if it is good enough for the NYSE, it's probably a safe bet among marijuana stocks. In addition, IIPR has a highly experienced management team that has a proven track record of outperforming in the REIT space.

Strategy

As the company's home page says, "We target medical-use cannabis facilities for acquisition, including sale-leaseback transactions, with tenants that are licensed growers under long-term triple-net leases. We believe this industry is poised for significant growth in coming years, and we are focused on being a creative capital provider to this industry through the long-term ownership of cultivators' mission-critical facilities."

Their acquisition strategy is to act as a source of capital to licensed growers of medical marijuana by acquiring and leasing back their real estate locations. By leasing their properties back from IIPR, growers have the opportunity to redeploy the capital from the sale into their company's core operations.

Acquisitions

In 2017, Innovative Industrial successfully acquired PharmaCannis property in New York. This created great revenue and the company got an impressive 17.2% cap rate. A few months later, IIPR entered a purchase agreement for a 72,000 square foot medical marijuana facility in Capitol Heights, Maryland. The building is still under construction and will be leased on a NNN basis to Holistic Industries LLC.

Like the PharmaCannis property, this Maryland property will have three revenue streams for Innovative. This includes a base rent of 15% of the total amount IIPR invests-- higher than Pharmacannis' 12.7% of the purchase price. It will grow at 3.25% per year. IIPR will also collect a property management fee of 1.5% of base rent-- same as the Pharmacannis lease. Lastly, as rent reserve, IIPR will collect $1.9 per year from Holistic and $1.265 million per year for the first five years from Pharmacannis. (seekingalpha.com)

Conclusion

At the time of this writing, IIPR looks to be only breaking even for 2017. However, with its successful strategy in place, experienced leadership and lack of competition, a few more deals like the ones above will make for a stellar 2018.

Visit innovativeindustrialproperties.com/ for more current information.

Company Highlights

Market Capitalization: $67.9 M

Shares Outstanding: 3.5 M

Price / Earnings: 69.82

Net Profit Margin: 21.09%

Return on Equity: 9.23%

Revenue: N/A

Industry: Real Estate Investment Trusts

Share Price 52 Week Range: $14.50 - 20.52

Company Profile

Address: 17190 Bernardo Center Drive, San Diego, CA 92128

Phone: 858-997-3332

Number of Employees: N/A

Chief Executive Officer, President & Director: Paul Smithers

Executive Chairman: Alan Gold

Chief Financial Officer: Robert Sistek

6. MedReleaf Corp. (LEAF:TSE) (OTCQB: MEDFF)

Founded in 2013, MedReleaf is yet another Canadian licensed producer dedicated to patient care, scientific innovation, research and advancing the understanding of the therapeutic benefits of cannabis.

MedReleaf delivers varied high quality products to patients seeking safe and effective medical marijuana. It especially has a high market share in the cannabis oil space, therefore their products appeal to the more affluent. This is because cannabis oils have a higher price point and margin than dried cannabis.

Earnings

For a company that just went public on May 2017, MedReleaf has already given its shareholders a nice return. It has been consistently profitable for the past two years. Their revenue rose from $19,302,000 to $40,339,000 year over year in the period till March 2017, a 109% annual increase. This is a sizable surge for any stock-- even compared to a cannabis stock.

Furthermore, after adding new cannabis extracts into their portfolio of products, their revenue grew to $10,416,000 from $8,804,000 and their net income grew over four times, for the quarter till June 2017. Their diversifying portfolio should help MedReleaf continue to grow their revenue throughout 2018. (seekingalpha.com)

Expansion

The primary purpose of MedReleaf's IPO was to finance its expansion plans, especially at its Bradford facility in Ontario. Since then, it has ventured into new markets such as Brazil where it made its first export in August 2017. Their export was in response to a bid to treat a girl- Sofia Langenbach- who suffered from severe refractory epilepsy and seizures. As it did with the children in Mexico, her seizures could only be alleviated by the use of cannabis oil.

MedReleaf also prides itself in participating in ground-breaking research and development projects. For instance, the company recently made a deal with Flora Fotonica Ltd. They will invest and collaborate on the development of specialized grow lighting systems for marijuana cultivation. In return, Flora Fotonica will provide MedReleaf with exclusive access to its proprietary LED lighting technology. (fool.ca)

Conclusion

With an ever growing market cap of over $800M, clear vision and strong brand, MedReleaf's stellar growth trajectory is expected to continue into 2018 and serve as a good bet for investors looking for healthy gains.

Visit medreleaf.com for more current information.

Company Highlights

Market Capitalization: $812.3 B

Shares Outstanding: 90.5 M

Price / Earnings: 67.84

Revenue: N/A

Industry: Pharmaceuticals

Share Price 52 Week Range: $5.86 - 9.32

Company Profile

Address: P.O. Box 3040, Markham, ON, Canada L3R 6G4

Phone: +1-289-317-1000 x1041

Number of Employees: N/A

President & Co-Founder: Eitan Popper

CEO & Co-Founder: Neil J. Closner

Chief Financial Officer: Igor Gimelshtein

7. Cronos Group, Inc. (CVE:MJN) (OTC:PRMCF)

Formerly known as PharmaCan Capital Corp, Cronos Group Inc. invests in firms which are licensed to produce and sell medical marijuana. Its portfolio includes In The Zone, Peace Naturals, Whistler Medical Marijuana Co., ABcann, Hydropothecary, Vert Medical, and Evergreen Medicinal Supply. Its Peace Naturals subsidiary is already exporting to Germany.

The company was founded by Lorne Michael Gertner and Paul Rosen on August 21, 2012 and is headquartered in Toronto, Canada.

Earnings

Most recently in 2017, Cronos' strong operational strategy resulted in a 25% increase in sales quarter over quarter: $643k in Q2 from $514k in Q1. Overall, the quarter produced $174,879 in positive net income with a realized $1.3M gain in net income from non-core investments.

Domestic sales contributed 77% to the topline in the quarter. During the quarter, the company commanded a domestic average selling price of $9.50 per gram. In addition, the Cost of Goods Sold continued to decline to $2.18 per gram in Q2 after many operational upgrades. Management expects COGS to continue to decline as two of their facilities ramp up production.

Note, Cronos Group is raising cash at the expense of its shareholders who'll find their existing shares diluted in value. Since its birth in 2013, the company's share count has grown from about 12 million to more than 125 million by 2017. Furthermore, its accumulated deficit, an aggregate of all of its quarterly losses, has increased to roughly $5.6 million. (fool.com)

Nevertheless, market analysts project outstanding earnings growth in 2018, supported by equally strong sales. Profit growth, coupled with smart aggressive expansion will likely be the future for MJN.

Investments

Cronos Group owns a 21.5% stake in Whistler Medical Marijuana Corp, a licensed producer in Canada whose entire product line is 100% certified organic. Cronos recently announced that WMMC had been granted an affirmation letter from Health Canada regarding the company's announced 65,000 square foot expansion in Pemberton, British Columbia. With interest in five other Licensed Producers and two LP applicants, Cronos Group is focused on building an impressive brand portfolio. (thecronosgroup.com)

Cronos also formed a partnership with Pedanios to export cannabis to Germany. In an interview on Bezinga.com, CEO Michael Gorenstein stated, "We see Germany and other places in Europe as extremely attractive [markets] because cannabis is treated as a medicine. Like any other medicine, you receive a prescription for it from your doctor, and insurance is mandated to cover it," Gorenstein added. "That, I believe, is what separates it from other places where everyone is wondering when will recreational legalization come. I believe an insurance-covered medical market is at least as good, if not superior, to a recreational market."

MJN's diversification is a necessity as a principal investment company. While it clearly has a majority investment in Peace Naturals, which recently announced a 315,000-square-foot expansion that includes a 286,000-square-foot facility, Cronos also has a half-dozen other investments. This ensures that should problems arise at one company, like declining sales, Cronos Group can still lean on its other subsidiaries as a hedge. (seekingalpha.com)

Facility in Israel

In September 2017, Cronos announced it entered a strategic joint venture to establish a medical marijuana production facility in Israel. CEO Michael Gorenstein explained, "there are certain realities such as the cost of power and the climate that make it difficult to compete internationally on a cost level."

In Canada, producers need to use all kinds of synthetic automated systems and artificial lighting to create an outdoor environment suited for marijuana cultivation indoors. However, Israel has these conditions naturally with its sunlight and low humidity throughout the year. (newswire.ca)

Conclusion

In 2017, Cronos Group announced the company's recent recognition as the top performer in the 2017 TSX Venture 50. This award is reserved for the best performing publicly traded companies on the TSX Venture Exchange. In 2016, Cronos Group delivered the highest stock price appreciation in the Diversified Industries sector and has continued this momentum throughout 2017. (newswire.ca/)

Visit thecronosgroup.com for more current information.

Company Highlights

Market Capitalization: $352.3 M

Shares Outstanding: 143.8 M

Revenue: N/A

Industry: Agriculture

Share Price 52 Week Range: $0.29 - 2.84

Company Profile

Address: 76 Stafford Street, Suite 302, Toronto, ON M6J 2S1

Phone: 416-504-0004

Number of Employees: N/A

Chairman, Chief Executive Officer, President: Michael Gorenstein J.D.

Chief Financial Officer: William Hilson CPA

Chief Operating Officer: David Hsu

8. THC Biomed Intl Ltd (CNSX:THC) (OTC:THCBF)

As one of the smaller market cap stocks on this list, THC BioMed International is an authorized Canadian licensed producer of dried Medical Marijuana and Cannabis oil. THC engages in the research, development, and cultivation of medical cannabis. It also provides horticulture training, record keeping and documenting, research studies, and analytical services.

THC also intends to participate in a genetic exchange service that would enable producers to exchange strains with THC Biomed. This would increase its genetic bank while giving producers the ability to increase their strain supply. THC currently offers 29 different Genetic strains.

Ratios

The Price to book ratio is the current share price of a company divided by the book value per share. At the time of this writing, the Price to Book ratio for THC is 41.26091, signifying the stock might be undervalued, considering where its revenue is likely headed after Canada's legalization in July.

Similarly, Price to Cash flow ratio is another helpful ratio in determining a company's value. The Price to Cash Flow for THC is - 59.744016. This ratio is calculated by dividing the market value of a company by cash from operating activities.

Lastly, the price to earnings ratio is used to determine a company's profitability. The price to earnings ratio for THC Biomed is 275.757971. This ratio is found by taking the current share price and dividing by earnings per share. THC has a high number because it's a growth stock within an emerging industry. More established companies typically have a lower P/E. (www.nasdaq.com)

Low Prices

THC BioMed Intl Ltd recently announced that it is now authorized by Health Canada to sell dried marijuana to registered patients under the ACMPR.

John Miller, CEO of THC, "Our inventory is ready. Authorized customers can order from our new website www.thcbiomed.com and have products shipped directly to their homes... Our pricing structure reflects our mandate of supplying good quality marijuana at an affordable price... THC intends to soon begin selling dried marijuana as an interim supply to registered home growers at $4.20 per gram. We believe this would be the lowest price ever offered to medical patients in Canada. We are pleased to offer this wholesale-type pricing to our fellow growers. The home growing market is expected to expand rapidly in the event recreational marijuana is introduced."

Growth

Earlier in 2017, THC BioMed announced that it has entered into a capital commitment agreement with GEM Global Yield Fund LLC. This agreement is for a $10 million capital commitment from GEM. Proceeds raised from the investment will be used for working capital and general corporate purposes, such as the support of THC Biomed's ongoing activities, development and expansion as a Licensed Producer.

THC Biomed also announced that it has received an order to export dried cannabis to Germany. They have initiated the process to meet the regulatory requirements for exporting to the European Union, a potentially billion dollar cannabis market. (prnewswire.com)

Visit thcbiomed.com for more current information.

Company Highlights

Market Capitalization: $57.7 M

Shares Outstanding: 104.7 M

Revenue: N/A

Industry: Other Metals/Minerals

Share Price 52 Week Range: $0.24 - 1.45

Company Profile

Address: 888 Dunsmuir Street, Vancouver, British Columbia V6C 3K4

Phone: +1.604.608.6314

Number of Employees: N/A

President, Chief Executive Officer & Director: John Miller

Chief Financial Officer: Hee Jung Chun

Chief Capital Markets Officer: Damien E. Reynolds

Chief Accountant: Tracey A. St. Denis

9. Terra Tech Corporation (OTC:TRTC)

A favorite small cap stock in the United States, Terra Tech Corp. is a vertically integrated cannabis-focused agriculture company, which engages in cultivating and providing medical cannabis. Because production is vertically integrated, the company is involved in growing and processing the raw plant material, as well as selling the end product.

Founded in 2008 and headquartered in Newport Beach, CA, Terra Tech Corp is "pioneering the future by integrating the best of the natural world with technology to create sustainable solutions for medical cannabis production, extraction and distribution, plant science research and development, food production and Closed Environment Agriculture (CEA). Through this development, we have created relevant brands in both the cannabis and agriculture industries." (terratechcorp.com)

Multiple Subsidiaries

Terra Tech Corp. operates through multiple subsidiary businesses including: Blüm, IVXX Inc., Edible Garden, MediFarm LLC and GrowOp Technology. Through these subsidiaries, TRTC is committed to cultivating and providing the high quality medical cannabis consistently delivered to qualified, registered medical marijuana establishments.

Terra Tech's subsidiary, Blüm offers a broad selection of medical marijuana products including flowers and edibles throughout its California and Nevada locations. Subsidiary, IVXX, Inc. produces medical cannabis-extracted products for regulated medical cannabis dispensaries throughout California. The wholly-owned subsidiary,

Edible Garden, cultivates a premier brand of local and sustainably grown hydroponic produce, sold through major grocery stores such as ShopRite, Walmart, Kroger, and others throughout the East coast and the Midwest. MediFarm LLC is focused on medical cannabis cultivation and permitting businesses throughout Nevada. Lastly, the wholly-owned subsidiary GrowOp Technology, specializes in controlled environment agricultural technologies.

Revenue

Terra Tech Corp's revenue has been exploding over the last few years. Total revenue for the full year 2016 was $25.33 million. That is an increase of 154% from $9.98 million generated in 2015. The 2017 first quarter revenue alone was $6.82 million which is an increase of 340% compared to the prior year's first quarter. Year-over-year increase was due to revenue generated by Blüm open sales from Nevada dispensaries and the sale of proprietary high best products.

Terra Tech has seen significant revenue growth. Unfortunately, it has also seen net income losses as well, mainly due to its expansion projects. Terra Tech expanded its facilities throughout 2016. and 2017.

Expansion

On March 7, 2017 Terra Tech announced that it had executed a lease for 13,000 square feet of industrial space in Oakland. The company is working on completing a "state of the art cultivation facility projected to produce over one metric ton of premium grade cannabis per annum for its IVXX brand."

In the beginning of 2018, California will become an enormous market for recreational marijuana- a market legalized for all. TRTC will likely surge in value, even more than it did when Nevada legalized earlier in 2017. Of all the marijuana penny stocks, Terra Tech is set to benefit the most from legalization in Nevada and California.

Analysts expect Terra Tech's expansion to increase revenue even more in 2018. (seekingalpha.com)

Visit terratechcorp.com for more current information.

Company Highlights

Market Capitalization: $151.6 M

Shares Outstanding: 863.7 M

Revenue: $25.3 M

Industry: Agricultural Commodities/Milling

Share Price 52 Week Range: $0.14 - 0.54

Company Profile

Address: 4700 Von Karman, Newport Beach, California 92660

Phone: +1.855.447.6967

Number of Employees: 175

Chairman, President & Chief Executive Officer: Derek A. Peterson

Chief Operating Officer & Director: Kenneth Vande Vrede

Chief Financial Officer & Accounting Officer: Michael C. James

Secretary, Treasurer & Director: Michael A. Nahass

10. mCig Inc. (OTC: MCIG)

Another favorite penny stock in the United States is mCig Incorporated. mCIg is another fast-growing company, whose earnings reports keep growing at an outstanding pace. Headquartered in Beverly Hills and founded in 2010, the company operates through two divisions: mCig Construction and mCig Commercial.

The mCig Construction division develops, designs and constructs modular buildings with unique and proprietary elements that assist cannabis growers in the market. This full-service construction company currently operates in the Nevada market, but plans to expand once federal laws change.

The mCig Commercial division manufactures, distributes, and retails the mCig - an affordable loose-leaf eCig, which apparently provides a smoother inhalation experience. It offers electronic cigarettes and related products through its online store mcig.org, as well as through the company's wholesale, distributor, and retail programs. (mcig.org)

Revenue

The company has successfully expanded from generating e-cigarettes to various avenues for growth in the cannabis industry. Revenue for mCig grew 158% year over year to $4.5 million. Net income is also outstanding. It went from losses of $1.4 million to net income of $1.5 million for fiscal year 2017.

CEO Paul Rosenberg on Q3 2017 Results, "Last quarter was monumental for mCig, as we blew through the revenue ceiling and bolstered our balance sheet. Everyone should have a chance to read this quarter's financial report. The $2.1 million combination of $1.3 million in record operating revenues plus a non-recurring accounting revenue gain, which I will discuss in just a few minutes, has generated once again another record-breaking quarter. The $1.3 million operating income proves to our shareholders and management, we are doing great business and are on the right track. Our current quarter, the final quarter of this fiscal year is on track to be even better and put our full fiscal year revenue at around three times last year's $1.6 million. We will end our fiscal year with a substantial net earnings." (seekingalpha.com)

Supply Division Expands Operations in California

In late 2017, mCig reported that its supply segment, Cannabiz Supply had expanded its operations into California. Cannabiz introduced its operation in Temecula, California capitalizing on months of groundwork and will begin creating revenue ahead of its estimated implementation plan. The segment will be working with dispensaries and production facilities in fulfilling their supply needs for businesses throughout the vast California region. California will have legalized recreational marijuana in 2018.

Visit www.mcig.org for more current information.

Company Highlights

Market Capitalization: $54.4 M

Price / Earnings: 34.95

Shares Outstanding: 400.4 M

Revenue: $4.8 M

Industry: Industrial Machinery

Share Price 52 Week Range: $0.03 - 0.51

Company Profile

Address: 2831 St. Rose Parkway, Henderson, Nevada 89052

Phone: +1.571.426.0107

Number of Employees: 69

Chairman, President & Chief Executive Officer: Paul Rosenberg

Chief Financial Officer: Michael Hawkins

Chief Technology Officer: Patrick Lucey

Chief Research & Development Officer: Michael Snody

11. Auscann Holdings (ASX:AC8) (OTC:ACNNF)

Auscann Group Holdings was recently added to the Australian index ASX after completing a successful reverse takeover of TW Holdings. AusCann is well positioned to take advantage of the developing medical marijuana market because of its strong team. The team includes the experienced, Canadian pot producer, Canopy Growth Corporation (TSE:WEED) and Chilean medicinal cannabis grower Fundación Daya. Since its addition to the ASX, Auscann's stock price has more than quadrupled.

Canopy Growth Corp Partnership

Canopy supplies AusCann with knowledge and experience, not to mention product as AusCann's first harvest prepares for sale. In addition, Chile's Daya was the first company in Chile legally allowed to grow medical marijuana. With its team and management in place, AusCann intends to import cannabis products from Canopy Growth to meet the demand of Chile and Australia's many consumers. When combined, Chile and Australia's population is about equal to the population of Canada! (https://www.businessinsider.com)

Revenue Potential

Though it will be a while before Auscann can generate revenue worth mentioning, analysts have postulated its potential just based on the population of those with chronic pain. If AusCann could command just 5% of the $5.8 billion chronic pain treatment market, it could generate sales of $290 million. This would justify a market cap in excess of $1.1 billion, based on a price-to-sales ratio of 4.

Best-case scenario sees revenue generation commence in 2018 at the earliest, with significant generation in 2019. (seekingalpha.com)

Visit http://www.auscann.com.au/ for more information.

Company Highlights

Market Capitalization: $51.7 M

Shares Outstanding: 129.3 M

Revenue: N/A

Price / Earnings: 31.99

Industry: Biotech & Pharma

Share Price 52 Week Range: $0.17 - 0.75

Company Profile

Address: 2831 St. Rose Parkway, Henderson, Nevada 89052

Phone: +1.571.426.0107

Number of Employees: N/A

Chairman: Dr. Mal Washer

Managing Director: Elaine Darby

Executive Director: Harry Karelis

12. Kush Bottles Inc. (OTC: KSHB)

Headquartered in Santa Ana, CA, Kush Bottles, Inc. is the U.S.'s largest distributor of cannabis packaging, supplies, and accessories. Kush Bottles's activities include marketing and sale of packaging products and solutions to customers operating in the regulated medical and recreational cannabis industries. It offers a range of products including bottles, bags, tubes, and containers among local urban farmers, and in greenhouse growers, as well as branding services.

2017 Revenue Summary

Not even including the recent 4th quarter, Kush's revenue increased from $8.2M in 2016 to $10.2M in 2017. In 2017, Kush's revenue continues to increase at least 20% month to month. That is quite impressive considering marijuana's current illegal status at the federal level in the U.S. (nasdaq.com)

Hawaii and Puerto Rico

Most recently, Kush Bottles added distribution partners in Hawaii and Puerto Rico. The company's Hawaii distribution partner will service the island's dispensaries that provide products to registered patients. Hawaii's reciprocity program will also allow sales to medical marijuana patients from other states as long as they have valid cards. This is also true for Puerto Rico's distribution partner in Puerto Rico, which also has a reciprocity clause. (www.newcannabisventures.com)

PR and Hawaii could potentially be huge markets. According to the Hawaii Department of Business, Economic Development and Tourism, Hawaii had approximately 9 million tourists visit in 2016.

Visit www.kushbottles.com for more information.

Company Highlights

Market Capitalization: $121.2 M

Shares Outstanding: 58.5 M

Revenue: $8.2 M

Industry: Miscellaneous Commercial Services

Share Price 52 Week Range: $1.61 - 4.88

Company Profile

Address: 1800 Newport Circle, Santa Ana, California 92705

Phone: +1.714.243.4311

Number of Employees: 40

Chief Executive Officer, Secretary & Director: Nicholas Kovacevich

President & Chief Operating Officer: Ben Wu

Manager-Product: John Kovacevich

13. MMJ Phytotech Ltd. (ASX: MMJ) (OTC: MMJJF)

MMJ PhytoTech Limited is an Australian company established to be a pioneer in the development of Medical Cannabis Delivery Systems, initially to markets in Australia, Israel, Europe, USA and Canada that have regulated medical cannabis laws, as well as New Zealand, which is on the way to being regulated in the near future. A 2017 addition on the ASX exchange, MMJ Phytotech stock has more than doubled.

With its experienced board and management team, the company is developing an intellectual property portfolio with patent applications for medical cannabis delivery systems and controlled dosages, in conjunction with leading Israeli based research centers, utilizing decades of medical cannabis research.

The company has multiple licensing hurdles to still leap over despite the Australian government giving the green light to distribute its pot product. In addition, it has deals with cultivation facilities in Canada and clinical research facilities in Israel to deliver prototyping, human trials, international patents and licensing to international pharmaceutical companies in return for royalties. (www.bloomberg.com)

Harvest One Cannabis Inc Partnership

With access to capital within the Canadian market, MMJ finished a strategic corporate restructuring, with the establishment of TSX-V listed Harvest One Cannabis Inc. Through a reverse takeover, MMJ now has 60% ownership of Harvest One, with the majority of the 40% balance of Harvest One being held by institutional investors who participated in a capital raising of approximately CAD$25 million. The ownership of PhytoTech Therapeutics in Israel has fully remained with MMJ. The finalization of the transaction provided two fully funded brands in the fastest growing legal cannabis market worldwide. (mmjphytotech.com/au)

HL Pharma Pty Ltd.

Earlier in 2017, MMJ also announced that their Australian distribution partner, HL Pharma Pty Ltd., received approval for a medical cannabis importation license from Canada's Department of Health.

A spokesperson for the company says, "Perth-based MMJ PhytoTech Limited is focused on becoming a leading, large-scale cannabis producer, targeting direct supply to the growing Canadian medical and recreational markets."

Visit http://mmjphytotech.com.au/ for more current information.

Company Highlights

Market Capitalization: $59.8 M

Shares Outstanding: 209.9 M

Revenue: N/A

Industry: Miscellaneous Commercial Services

Share Price 52 Week Range: $0.26 - 0.34

Company Profile

Address: Suite 5 CPC, 145 Stirling Highway, Nedlands WA
Australia 6009

Phone: + 61 8 9389 3150

Number of Employees: N/A

Chief Executive Officer: Dr. Daphna Heffetz

Non-Executive Chairman: Peter Wall

Managing Director: Andreas Gedeon

14. Emblem Corporation (CVE:EMC) (OTC:EMMBF)

Emblem Cannabis is another Canadian licensed producer of medical cannabis, with dedicated growers providing patients with premium cannabis strains. It has three businesses that cover the full cannabis spectrum:

1) Emblem produces and sells medical cannabis for qualified patients.

2) Emblem Pharmaceutical is exploring the ways patients can ingest this medicine.

3) And Grow Wise Health is providing cannabis education for both patients and physicians alike.

John Stewart, CEO Emblem Pharmaceutical Division, states, "Cannabinoids and other components of marijuana have real therapeutic value. Emblem is identifying the marijuana strains with the greatest evidence of benefit in various conditions, cultivating those strains at medical grade and developing advanced dosage forms to provide patients with accurate, consistent, high quality and convenient to use cannabis formulations."

Quarterly Financials for 2017

In 2017, Emblem has already past its total gross income for 2016 of $1.78M. As a young company, this is not hard to do. However, quarter to quarter in 2017 has seen more sluggish, but fair progress.

In the quarter ending in June, Emblem reported revenue of $538M. Within this same period, costs of goods dropped to $1.37M (from $1.62M in the previous quarter).

Expansion

A few days after being listed, the company announced that it was sitting on a cash pile of $27 million that it was looking to deploy in its expansion projects. Not long after, it got a go-ahead from Health Canada to begin production of cannabis oil. (newswire.ca)

By the end of 2017, Emblem Corp broke ground on newly acquired land, approximately 80 acres within the Company's current production facilities in Paris, Ontario. Emblem is building a 100,000sq. ft. state-of-the-art facility, with 60,000 sq. ft. dedicated to production and the remaining 40,000 sq. ft. allocated to support services and administrative functions. Once operational, Emblem expects this facility to produce up to 20,000 kilograms of dried cannabis. That's potentially $160.0 million in potential sales according to analysts. (globenewswire.com)

Visit http://emblemcorp.com/ for more current information.

Company Highlights

Market Capitalization: $89.4 M

Shares Outstanding: 71.6 M

Price / Earnings: 67.84

Revenue: N/A

Industry: Pharmaceuticals

Share Price 52 Week Range: $1.15 - 3.81

Company Profile

Address: PO Box 20087 Northville, Paris, ON N3L 4A5

Phone: +1 (416) 962-3300

Number of Employees: N/A

CEO Emblem Pharmaceutical Division: John Stewart

15. Medical Marijuana, Inc. (OTC: MJNA)

Another U.S. penny stock with amazing potential, Medical Marijuana Inc. engages in the provision of various business management solutions to the hemp and medical marijuana industries. It is comprised of a diversified portfolio of products, services, technology and businesses solely focused on the cannabis and hemp industries. The company was founded in 2003 and is headquartered in Poway, CA.

With a current market cap value of $221.5M, MJNA has a reserve of $755K of cash on the books, which compares with about $808K in total current liabilities. MJNA is seeing major top-line growth, with y/y quarterly revenues growing at 230.5%.

Latin American Influence

With the approval of MJNA's product Real Scientific Hemp Oil, Brazil became the first Latin American country to approve prescriptions for a medical cannabis product. In addition, a THC-free version of this Hemp Oil was also the first medical cannabis product accepted into Mexico when it was approved as a prescription medication early in 2016. It was authorized for a young girl Grace, who suffered up to 400 seizures a day. Although Mexico had approved the use of CBD for patients with a doctor's prescription, the government remained opposed to products with even trace amounts of THC in them. In order to import their CBD hemp oil to Mexico, MJNA had to develop a product completely free of THC and it succeeded. (medicalmarijuanainc.com)

Later in 2017, HempMeds Mexico opened its first office in Mexico. The announcement received international media attention during the

July 28, 2017 inauguration of the office in Monterrey, Nuevo Leon, Mexico. Medical Marijuana, Inc. CEO Dr. Stuart Titus stated, "We appreciate the outpouring of support that we received at the opening of the first HempMeds® Mexico office in Monterrey, Mexico, which reflects a growing demand for the Company's zero-Tetrahidrocannabidiol (THC) Real Scientific Hemp Oil-X™ (RSHO-X™). The extensive coverage that we received from both local and international media is a testament to the worldwide interest in cannabis reform happening in Mexico, and the efforts of HempMeds® Mexico to provide products for this rapidly expanding CBD hemp oil market."

In May 2016, Real Scientific Hemp Oil became the first medical cannabis product approved and imported for use in Paraguay. This event marked the third time in a little over a year that RSHO was the first cannabis product approved in a Latin American country.

More recently in October 2017, HempMeds Brazil gained media attention in Brazilian newspapers after a Federal judge there ordered the government to subsidize payments for Real Scientific Hemp Oil for a Brazilian citizen.

Kannaway Subsidiary

In late 2017, Medical Marijuana Inc reported the largest revenue quarter in its history, as well as the largest sales month and quarter for wholly owned subsidiary Kannaway. This included a gross revenue increase from $1,660,633 in 2016 to $6,131,415 in 2017, a quarter-over-quarter increase of 269%! MJNA also saw year-to-date and year-over-year revenue increase from $3,177,103 to $9,651,088 an increase of 203%.

Kannaway® CEO Blake Schroeder stated, "We are confident that Kannaway® is on a trajectory that continues to exceed expectations. We are proud to be a part of the Medical Marijuana, Inc. family, which actively supports efforts to increase access to cannabidiol (CBD) products worldwide."

Invite to United Nations

On November 4, 2017, MJNA made headlines when CFN Media Group discussed the company's invite to the United Nations.

CEO Dr. Stuart Titus stated, "We are honored and excited to speak to United Nations leaders on a global stage about CBD as a supplement aimed to maintain and improve the wellbeing of millions. We hope to bring light to the many benefits of CBD and convince decision-makers that CBD in its natural botanical state, derived from hemp, should be classified as a supplement."

Company of Firsts

Medical Marijuana, Inc. bills itself as a company of firsts. After all, it was the first publicly traded cannabis company in the United States in 2010. MJNA is also the first U.S. marijuana company to establish a global pipeline to other countries, especially Mexico, Brazil and Paraguay. According to their website, MJNA was also the first to introduce cannabis foods and supplements across U.S. state lines and international borders.

To see their other firsts, visit http://www.medicalmarijuanainc.com/

Company Highlights

Market Capitalization: $221.5 M

Shares Outstanding: 3.2 B

Revenue: $9.2 M

Industry: Biotech/ Pharma

Share Price 52 Week Range: $0.06 - 0.27

Company Profile

Address: 12255 Crosthwaite Circle, Poway, California 92064

Phone: +1.866.273.8502

Number of Employees: 39

Chairman & Chief Operating Officer: Michelle Sides

President, Chief Executive Officer & Director: Stuart W. Titus

Vice President-Operations: Blake Schroeder

Vice President-Business Development: Nick Massalas

16. Maricann Group Inc. (CNSX: MARI) (OTC: MRRCF)

Maricann Group, Inc. is a producer and distributor of medical cannabis. The company operates a cultivation, marijuana extraction and distribution business under federal license from the Government of Canada. Its products include Bubba Kush, Icann Oil, Forte 190, and MK Ultra. The company was founded in 2013 and is headquartered in Burlington, Canada.

Maricann's Aggressive Expansion

Despite its share price down-trending as of late, Maricann Group Inc is a $74.3 million company gaining a foothold in international markets. Its strong expansion strategy includes a bid to venture into Germany's large marijuana market. This started with a $42.5 million acquisition of 150,000 square feet of cultivation operations in a Ebersbach facility, as well as 250,000 square feet expansion of their two-tiered cultivation plan and outdoor hemp farm. Considering these acquisitions were made at a discount, they provided the company with a boost in asset valuation.

Maricann's CEO, Benjamin Ward states, "The Ebersbach facility offers Maricann a significant advantage in cost of overall construction and speed to market…. To construct a similar facility today, the estimated cost would be over 120 million EUR. Maricann entered into a reservation agreement to purchase the facility for a total price of 3,410,000 EUR at closing." (newcannabisventures.com)

Company Growth

Maricann has seen significant growth in their book value over the first two quarters of 2017. Their book value grew to $15.93 million in the second quarter of 2017 from their negative position of -$44.49 in the first quarter of 2017. This was due to the common stock acquired during this period. Unfortunately, revenue fell by 41% over the first two quarters in 2017 to $509,000 from $857,000, with cost of goods sold falling from $1.1 million to $195,000 within the same period. (fool.ca)

Conclusion

Despite its growing pains, Maricann has positioned itself as a global player, investing heavily in its bid to expand internationally. Analysts expect this company to be profitable as the world continues to accept marijuana as a viable commodity, especially Canada where it will be legalized across the board in mid-2018.

Company Highlights

Market Capitalization: $76.6 M

Shares Outstanding: 73.4 M

Revenue: N/A

Industry: Agriculture

Share Price 52 Week Range: $0.87 - 1.64

Company Profile

Address: 845 Harrington Court, Burlington, Ontario L7N 3P3

Phone: +844-627-4226

Number of Employees: N/A

Chief Operating Officer: James Hyssen

Chief Executive Officer & Director: Ben Ward

Vice President-Information Technology & Security: Stephen Lem

President: Terry Fretz

17. One World Cannabis Ltd. (OTC: OWCP)

Founded in 2014, One World Cannabis Ltd. is an Israeli company focused on the research and development of cannabis-based pharmaceuticals and treatments for a variety of ailments. The future goal of One World Cannabis is to be a leader in the research and development of cannabis based medicines and provide consulting services to governments looking to implement medical marijuana legislation.

OWC could be the next GW Pharmaceuticals. After all, there are only a handful of publicly-traded companies focused on cannabinoid-based, pharmaceutical development. In fact, as mentioned in the previous chapter, Israel is probably the best place in the world for cannabis research.

Unlike the U.S. government, the Israeli government has had few restrictions on doing research on cannabis, whether for the purpose of basic science or clinical studies. In fact, the Israeli government funds much of this research.

OWCP says that its research division "leverages the Company's extensive network comprising some of Israel's leading researchers, scientists, universities and hospitals, as well as cannabis breeders and extractors, to study and test the effectiveness of different combinations of cannabinoids in the treatment of disease and chronic conditions." (owcpharma.com)

Furthermore, OWCP's Chief Scientific Officer, Dr. Yehuda Baruch founded, implemented, and led the Israeli Medical Cannabis Unit under the Minister of Health for over 10 years. (insiderfinancial.com).

Strategic Relationship with Germany

In May 2017, OWC Pharmaceutical Research Corp. and German Innovation Partners (Mediq) announced a strategic agreement that will introduce OWCP's cannabinoid-based topical psoriasis cream to the German market. The agreement also includes scientific collaboration.

Based in Frankfurt, Mediq has the necessary experience and knowledge to bring cannabis products from Israel into European markets. Commenting on the collaboration with OWCP, Jan Wende, managing director of Mediq stated, "We're looking forward to initiating our efforts on behalf of OWCP in Europe, starting in our home market of Germany. Since German laws and regulations allow non-smokable forms of medical cannabis, we believe that OWCP's proprietary cannabinoid-based topical psoriasis cream is the right product at the right time. Furthermore, Germany is the largest European healthcare market and therefore offers the perfect platform to gain local evidence and roll out the concept into other European countries. Our initial focus for OWCP is on the German market, however we're excited about the long-term opportunities throughout Europe, a market with a population of over 740 million." (prnewswire.com)

Visit owcpharma.com/ for more current information.

Company Highlights

Market Capitalization: $46.3 M

Shares Outstanding: 146.3 M

Revenue: $50K

Industry: Pharmaceuticals

Share Price 52 Week Range: $0.06 - 3.23

Company Profile

Address: 22 Shaham Street, Petach Tikva, Tel Aviv 4918103

Phone: +972.3.770.4330

Number of Employees: N/A

Chairman, President & Chief Executive Officer: Mordechai Bignitz

Chief Financial Officer: Shmuel De-Saban

Chief Science Officer: Yehuda Baruch

18. ABcann Global Group (TSX-V: ABCN) (OTCQB: ABCCF)

Headquared in Canada, ABcann is a cost efficient producer of quality, organically grown, standardized plant based medicines. Though currently low on our list, Abcann is expected to rise fast in 2018 to be an international leader in the cannabis market. Subsidiary, ABcann Medicinals Inc. was one of the first companies to obtain a production license under the Marijuana for Medical Purposes Regulations.

Organic Marijuana

ABcann's flagship facility in Napanee, Ontario uses cutting-edge plant-growing technology to consistently produce organically grown and pesticide-free plants. In turn, these plants generate high-quality cannabis products. At the time of this writing, ABcann is expanding capacity to approximately 30,000 square feet. At the same time, ABcann is also opening a new 150,000 square foot facility in Napanee. ABcann is pursuing opportunities in Germany, Australia and other jurisdictions, as well as exploring the development of multiple delivery vehicles. (abcannglobal.com)

Product Line

In August 2017, ABcann Medicinals Inc. announced the release of a product with a high, yet legal CBD:THC (cannabidol:tetrahydrocannabinol) ratio. This is part of the company's strategy to provide a diverse range of products as it begins to sell cannabis oils to its customers. This product CBD-Med has a ratio of 27.6:1 (18.5% CBD to 0.67% THC). This is one of Canada's highest CBD products under Health Canada regulations.

ABcann has made available to patients a 1-1 THC/CBD drop, a high THC dropper and a high CBD dropper. This is in addition to ABcann's current high CBD products: NC:Med - 18.9:1 (18.9%

CBD to 1% THC) and DC:Med - 15.4:1 (15.4% CBD to 1% THC). Expect capsule products and soft gels to arrive shortly.

"The development of these products is in line with ABcann's corporate strategy as a premium product provider of organic, pesticide free cannabis," says Ken Clement, Executive Chairman of ABcann. "As the Company continues to scale production capacity, our product line will expand as we strive to increase shareholder value through capturing a larger market share of the current global medical markets." (Globe Newswire)

Expansion

On August 29, 2017, ABcann Global Corporation released the company's financial results for the quarter ending June 30, 2017. The first half of 2017 included a noteworthy expansion of its production capacity at both its Vanluven and Kimmett locations, using $40 million in working capital.

Aaron Keay, Chief Executive Officer of ABcann states, "We expect that the increase in production capacity will enable ABcann to increase the sales of our premium, organically grown, pesticide free cannabis products in the current domestic market and position the Company for global distribution in the emerging markets we have targeted. Further, the ability to serve larger and broader markets as a result of the production increase positions ABcann extremely well for the anticipated adult consumer market in July 2018."

Lastly, ABcann recently announced a strategic partnership agreement with Cannabis Wheaton Income Corp. ("CBW") that includes a $30m investment into ABcann. When this initial $30m equity placement is completed, CBW will have the opportunity to finance a 50,000 square foot expansion facility in a 50/50 joint venture. (abcannglobal.com)

Company Highlights

Market Capitalization: $75.6 M

Shares Outstanding: 99.6 M

Revenue: N/A

Industry: Agriculture

Share Price 52 Week Range: $0.62 - 1.25

Company Profile

Address: PO Box 157, Napanee, Ontario, K7R 3M3

Phone: +1-855-322-2266

Number of Employees: N/A

Chief Executive Office: Barry Fisherman

Chief Financial Officer: Jenny Guan

President, Opertations: Neil Kapp

19. OrganiGram Holdings Inc. (CVE:OGI) (OTCQB:OGRMF)

Like the licensed producers above, OrganiGram Holdings, Inc. also engages in the production and sale of medical marijuana in Canada. OrganiGram was founded on July 5, 2010 and is headquartered in Vancouver, Canada.

If its recent earnings are any indication, Organigram has not held up since its product recall in 2016. While the company's fast response to the recall had satisfied most shareholders, Organigram needs to do more to strengthen its brand in the eyes of customers.

Revenue

In this year's edition, OrganiGram fell considerably down our list, mostly due to its latest earnings. Net sales increased from $1.8 million in the third quarter of 2016 to around $1.9 million in the third quarter of 2017. This is a paltry increase in sales, especially in comparison to other Canadian producers on our list. For instance, Canopy Growth Corp increased its revenue in the third quarter of 2017 by 191% when compared to the same quarter in 2016.

Furthermore, Organigram had a profit of $367,720 in the third quarter of 2016. In the same quarter of 2017, the company reported a loss of $2,345,586, as well as a decline in grams of dried marijuana sold.

Based on these results, it seems the recall has tainted their reputation causing adverse effects on Organigram's business model. This is troubling for investors who are searching for companies which can actively increase their marijuana sales in preparation for legalization

of recreational marijuana in Canada in 2018.
(newcannabisventures.com)

Significant Growth

On the plus side, Organigram reported a 25% increase in registered patients from year to year. This is a positive indication that despite the recall, Organigram can continue to grow a sizable customer base of patients who will buy its cannabis. Another plus was the sale of around 190 liters of cannabis oil compared to 0 liters the previous year.

Certified Organic Product

Interestingly, what sets Organigram apart from other licensed producers is the fact they produce a certified organic product. With pot eventually becoming a commodity (like wheat) in Canada, being certified organic differentiates Organigram's marijuana as a superior product with limited competition. In addition, since an organic producer is required to keep comprehensive records, this will appeal to doctors who will likely have more confidence prescribing an organic product to their patients.

Organigram remains one of the top cannabis plays for investors. Visit http://www.organigram.ca for more current information.

Company Highlights

Market Capitalization: $228.1 M

Shares Outstanding: 104.6 M

Price / Earnings: N/A

Revenue: $4.6 M

Net Profit Margin: -150.73%

Industry: Agricultural Commodities/ Milling

Share Price 52 Week Range: $1.35 - 3.35

Company Profile

Address: 35A English Drive, Moncton, New Brunswick E1E 3X3

Phone: +1.647.453.8955

Number of Employees: N/A

Chief Executive Officer: Greg Engel

Independent Director & Chief Operating Officer: Larry Rogers

Chief Financial Officer: Peter R. Hanson

Director-Investor & Media Relations: Giselle Doiron

20. Teva Pharmaceuticals Industries Ltd. (NYSE: TEVA) (ADR)

Headquartered in Petah Tikva, Israel, Teva Pharmaceutical Industries Ltd. is a major multinational pharmaceutical company. Its current share price is down at $13.32 with a nice current dividend of 8.30%.

Cannabis Inhaler

In a world's first, Teva Pharmaceutical Industries Ltd. and Tel Aviv-based Syqe Medical signed an agreement in 2017 to market medical cannabis in an inhaler. Under the agreement, Teva will be the exclusive marketer and distributor of the inhaler. Syqe Medical says its inhaler will allow cannabis to be regarded as a standard medical treatment. In addition, the inhaler will allow medical professionals to prescribe a precise dose of cannabis, alleviating the patient's symptoms while minimizing psychoactive effects. Lastly, much like the oils do, the inhaler provides a convenient and accessible option for patients who are reluctant to smoke cannabis. (timesofisrael.com)

Bullish Case for 2018

Teva's stock price dived over the last year after its flagship drug Copaxone lost its exclusivity. Earnings estimates may continue to suffer as market share continues to shrink and become more competitive. However, analysts argue the 25% market share drop in Copaxone does not equal the 65% decline in stock value in 2017. Price is ridiculously low considering 3.5 Forward Earnings.

Being the largest manufacturer of generics, Teva has an advantage by having its operations vertically integrated allowing it to easily push drugs through its pipeline. In addition, besides Teva having a profound market share of around 25% in the world, it is also deeply tied to the State of Israel. This all means it's too big to fail.

Lastly, it has over 100 products planned to launch in 2018 this year (with nearly 600 generic medicines available). And it's also shedding assets to lessen its $35 billion in debt burden.

Visit tevapharm.com for more current information.

Company Highlights

Market Capitalization: $13.5 B

Shares Outstanding: 1.0 B

Current Dividend / Yield: $0.085 / 8.30%

Price/ Earnings: N/A

Revenue: $22.0 B

Industry: Pharmaceuticals

Share Price 52 Week Range: $13.26 - 44.13

Company Profile

Address: 5 Basel Street, Petach Tikva, Tel Aviv 49131

Phone: +972.3.926.7267

Number of Employees: 56,960

President & Chief Executive Officer: Yitzhak Peterburg

President & CEO-Global Operations: Carlo de Notaristefani

Chief Financial Officer & Group Executive VP: Eyal Desheh

President-Global Research & Development: Michael R. Hayden

Researching Companies

The companies listed in the last chapter all have great potential to be profitable investments for you. As these companies mature, keep studying their metrics to determine if they remain worth holding. Furthermore, since performance can change in time, you may have to consider companies beyond this list. And you should. After all, every month there are more publicly traded cannabis companies added to exchanges around the world.

In the ever-changing landscape of the stock market, it's important for investors to learn how to appropriately choose a stock to invest in. The waters get murkier when the pool of stocks you are checking out are growth stocks. This is because growth stocks will more often than not use their capital for expansion projects, which will result in their fundamentals showing debt and negative cash flow.

Below are tips on how to evaluate and research growth stocks in this sector or any other sector. When studying these guidelines, it helps to look beyond numbers and remind yourself you are buying a piece of this company. Therefore, wouldn't you like to be as educated as possible on everything there is to know about the company?

Also keep in mind, even if the company is not in your country, we live in an age where the internet can provide nearly all the information you need. Even the smallest of companies has plenty of information online if you dig enough.

Study Outstanding Shares

A key metric that is often overlooked is the number of shares outstanding. **Outstanding shares** refer to a company's stock currently held by all its shareholders. For instance, a typical new trader might view Company X as more valuable than Company Y, simply because X has a higher share price. Let's assume they have the same market cap of $100M too. Now, when you consider each company's outstanding shares, you would observe company X has 1 billion outstanding shares, in comparison to company Y, which has only 1 million outstanding shares.

Sometimes through a secondary offering or share issuance to raise capital, a company might dilute its shares. This means the number of shares outstanding can often balloon out of control. Through stock splits or through secondary offerings, it often dilutes the ownership percentage held by holding investors. The trade-off, though, is that the company gets to keep the cash raised, which increases its overall value.

When a company whose stock you own dilutes its shares, your first move should be to figure out whether you think the price the company will get for its shares reflects its fair value. If the company is getting a good deal, then that's positive. If not, you may want to lessen or close your position. Another possibility is that an insider is selling their large position, which might suggest a bad sign too.

Share issuance isn't necessarily bad, but they do require due diligence. Understanding the motivation behind them is important in order to make the right move.

Revenue Growth

Revenue growth alone is often not the best metric for growth stocks. While studying the average revenue growth of a company for the previous few years can be helpful, an investor should also look at the potential profitability of the company. To do this, an investor should study the company's losses, debt, financing, efficient use of capital, brand recognition, etc.

Financing

A company closing a round of financing at around current stock prices is positive news. After all, the more capital raised, the greater the odds of success-- especially if the investors themselves are reputable. For instance, Canadian unicorn, Canopy Growth Corp. owns a considerable amount of newbie AusCann Holdings. This shows investors around the world that AusCann is a legit company.

Even though financing is usually a positive sign, it can be negative as well. For instance, if a company closes a financing deal at a 70% discount to market price, it's almost certain they are desperate for money. Therefore, when you do your due diligence, establish what price the financing took place. If a company raises money at too great of a discount to the current stock price, it's also a sign the current price is probably overvalued.

Profitability

In order to grow, a growth stock needs capital. Besides borrowing money, most capital comes from profits. In order for these companies to expand, they need to sometimes spend quite a bit. It's because of this that these companies will not be offering dividends any time soon.

Earnings Per Share

A great metric to understand a company's profitability is earnings per share (EPS). EPS shows how a company's profits are allocated to each share. This will reveal the per-share allocation of a company's profits.

EPS is used in calculating price/earnings ratio (P/E). Keep in mind, while an established company might have a P/E of around 25, a growth stock will often have a much higher P/E since its funds are often used for expansion and keeping the lights on.

Operating Margin and Net Margin

Two popular metrics for researching growth stocks are operating margin and net margin.

Operating margin is a measurement of what percentage of a company's revenue is left over after paying for variable costs of production such as raw materials, and wages. Consequently, it becomes a great measure of a company's management, since it reveals how they are controlling operating costs.

Net margin is the percentage of revenue remaining after all operating expenses have been deducted from a company's total revenue. These expenses include interest and taxes.

Both metrics are especially useful when compared to industry and competitor's averages. Furthermore, an investor should consider how these measures are trending over previous years. Strong growth in these numbers show financial stability and extra working capital.

Efficient Use of Capital

Investors also need to examine how a company uses its capital for the company's best interests, like market share or new products. Two excellent metrics are ROA (return on assets) and ROE (return on equity). Both numbers are designed to show how effectively a company utilizes its current assets to generate additional profits.

ROA

Displayed as a percentage, return on assets is calculated by dividing a company's net earnings by its total assets. The higher the return, the more efficient management is in utilizing its asset base. For instance, ROA ratio for notable, established companies like General Electric and Microsoft are 2.3% and 18.0% respectively. However, a growth penny stock may have a considerably smaller figure.

ROE

ROE or "return on net worth" is calculated by taking the net income and dividing it by the total shareholders' equity. This will show how effectively a company generates a return on the capital provided by investors. If the company retains these profits, the common shareholders will only realize this gain by having an appreciated stock.

Best way to track a company's progress and earnings, is to calculate ROE and ROA at the beginning of a period and at the end of a period to see the change in return. There is hardly a magic number you should be looking for here. Instead, compare these numbers to industry averages, and you'll get an idea where this company stands among its competitors.

Competitive Advantage

Comparing the metrics above with other companies is one way to discover a company's competitive advantage. Other ways to garner this important quality include comparing ability to keep costs low in production, brand recognition, even the date the company started, etc.

Brand Recognition

However, there are other factors that aren't as measurable. A big one is brand recognition, which is the extent to which a consumer can correctly identify a particular product only by its logo, tag line, packaging, etc. For instance, Canopy Growth Corp. has 'WEED' as its ticker symbol on the Toronto Stock Exchange. This is great branding, since a ticker symbol like this can easily get the attention of investors looking to get in the "weed game".

Location

Another competitive advantage could be the location of a company's facilities or operations. In regards to producing marijuana, it's much more advantageous to be a company based near states where cannabis is legal, as opposed to states that aren't. For instance, Terra Tech Corporation has a competitive advantage, since its operations are based near most of the states that recently voted for recreational marijuana legalization.

Partnerships and Contracts

Partnerships and contracts, especially with big companies, offer a big competitive advantage as well. As mentioned in the last chapter, AusCann's share price has done so well partly because of its affiliations with major companies in Canada and Brazil. Same can be said for Canopy Growth's operations in Germany, or Medical Marijuana Inc's partnerships with Mexico.

In addition, contracts with celebrities can be huge for brand recognition. Canopy Growth Corp. jumped to record high prices after unveiling a line of marijuana products for the domestic market in a partnership with rapper, Snoop Dogg.

Analyst Coverage and Conference Calls

While plenty of analyst coverage is bogus, it is still a good policy to pay attention. It will often impact a stock. Though most qualified analysts will not cover penny stocks, they will often cover marijuana penny stocks because of how hot they are. The winners and losers in this industry can be made or broken based on analysts coverage. Articles on breakthrough contract wins or earnings reports are often big news. If an analyst does write an article, pay attention how it affects the company in question.

Same goes for conference calls. Companies will usually announce them anywhere from the day before to a few weeks ahead of time. Positive conference calls can really separate the winners from the losers, so pay attention.

SEC Suspensions or Halts

When following companies, you may hear of SEC trading suspensions or halts. With penny stocks especially, these things happen, usually after big pump and dump-induced runups or other forms of manipulation. SEC (The Securities and Exchange Commission) is a government commission created by the United States Congress with goals of protecting investors, maintaining fair and orderly functioning of securities markets, and facilitating capital formation.

Many penny stocks, including many marijuana stocks, don't file with the SEC. If you're investing in a company's stock that doesn't file with the SEC, it's better to dump them. There's probably a good reason they aren't reporting and it's simply not worth it to you to hold onto their shares. A lot of manipulation happens in the stock market, but especially with penny stocks in a burgeoning industry like this one with many competitors. Investors can reference the SEC's EDGAR database to see if a company files with the SEC.

By checking SEC filings, investors can verify information they've heard about the company. Also, these filings can offer a hidden store of insight, but that insight only matters if it's been independently audited by accountants. For instance, if looking at filings, you notice the company has changed its name four times in five years, that's a red flag signaling a potentially terrible trade.

Lawsuits

Investors should also investigate company's lawsuits. A company being sued is not a reason for panic and to close all your shares. But why is it being sued? If a company made a mistake and is immediately rectifying the situation, it still may be worth holding onto the stock, especially if your investment was made for the long term. After all, a few of the leading licensed producers in the Canadian exchange have already been sued, such as Canopy Growth Corp. and Organigram. It's sometimes just the price of business.

Nevertheless, it is a wise policy to pay attention. Sometimes a company is sued for reasons that reveal the company's illegitimacy. Either way, lawsuits will often greatly affect the share price.

In Conclusion

To find the most promising companies in this heap of promising companies, investors need to look hard into every aspect of a company and its coverage by the media. Investors should analyze a variety of angles that provide glimpses into its efficiency, plans for the future, profitability, industry reputation, competitive advantages and disadvantages.

Finally, never forget that the cannabis industry is still growing in conjunction with regulations and an always-evolving legislation throughout the world. Deviations are to be expected. As is true throughout the markets, nothing is a forgone conclusion. Even thoughtful investing in this burgeoning market can be riskier than usual, but it's also incredibly exciting and potentially hugely rewarding.

Stock Trading Strategies

As mentioned earlier, this book assumes you have experience as a stock trader. It will not be going into detail about stock terms, such as short selling, limit prices and stop losses. Nor will the book get into the details of studying charts when conducting technical analysis. You're going to have to learn about those elsewhere. While these can be simple terms by definition, they can be very complicated and go beyond the scope of this book. However, there's mountains of information on how to use them online. Instead, this chapter will focus on general trading concepts to use for the kind of growth stocks covered in this book.

Just a reminder, any industry still in its infancy has many risks in regards to investing. As an example, just study the dot com bubble that bursts in the early 2000's. The risk associated with trading marijuana stocks means that they might be best suited for the more aggressive, seasoned investor. If you are a more conservative trader, it may be worth it to you to wait and see how the industry plays out in several years, though you will indeed miss its largest profits.

Designing Your Strategy

Your stock trading strategy should obviously be designed so that you can trade successfully. Your strategy should allow you to enter and exit trades in anticipation of price changes in the market.

Compare stock trading to playing chess, in that successful chess players design strategies specific to the types of opponents they may face. They anticipate their opponent's moves based upon their chosen strategy. And they play offense and defense. As a trader you must not only use defensive moves to protect your capital, but use offensive moves in order to grow capital through profitable trades.

When you design a strategy, important factors to consider include:

- Type of Trader You Are

- The Amount of Available Capital

- When to Enter and Exit Trades

Type of Trader You Are

What kind of trader you are largely depends on your risk tolerance. If you are more risk averse, a buy and hold strategy with companies you like is your best bet.

Buy and Hold Strategy

The buy-and-hold strategy ignores short term movements of share price. Instead, the investor concentrates on the long term. He or she believes that price movements over the long term will outweigh the price movements in the short term.

Active Trading Strategy

Active traders, however, believe that short-term volatility of share prices are where the profits are made. There are various ways to accomplish an active-trading strategy. Besides the VERY active trading strategies known as 'Day Trading' and 'Scalping', there are two other types of active trading that are not quite as dependent on volatility and therefore, better suited for the long term success of this sector.

1. Position Trading

Position traders (or Trend traders) look to determine the direction of the market, but they do not try to forecast any price action. Typically, trend traders jump on the trend after it has established itself, and when the trend breaks, they usually close their position. Position trading requires that investors discover the trend through fundamental analysis (news) and/ or technical analysis (charts). In essence, trend traders look for successive higher highs or lower highs in price action to determine the trend of a stock.

For instance, when Trump's administration told the press they would likely be taking action against the states that had legalized recreational marijuana, it put all marijuana stocks on a temporary downtrend-- even pot stocks on foreign exchanges. If you are a position trader, this would have been a time to lessen your positions until the trend ended.

2. Swing Trading

On the other hand, swing traders enter at the end of trends. How? Well there is often volatility at the end of a trend when it's about to reverse itself. In addition, the news can create new trends-- such as earnings reports or conference calls. For instance, when Canada begins to implement its cannabis legalization through a set of laws in 2018, it will likely create an uptrend. At this time, an investor would add to those positions.

The Amount of Available Capital

An investor should never trade without adequate capital. Just like the companies you're trading, not having enough capital in relation to the trades you make can often lead to trouble. It's poor risk and money management.

The amount of working capital that you will need depends on a number of factors. Some of those factors include: Capital Requirement for Diversification, Capital Requirement for Dollar Cost Averaging, Your Trading Goals and Margin Requirements.

Capital Requirement for Diversification

For instance, if you want to invest $10,000 in one stock, but have $15,000 total opening account balance, that will leave you only $5,000 to invest in other stocks. This would be very poor diversification. Therefore, in order to diversify your portfolio more evenly and yet still hold a $10k position in that first stock, it's probably better to have a lot more capital-- say at least $100k available.

Capital Requirement for Dollar Cost Averaging

Dollar-cost averaging is an investment technique of buying a fixed amount of shares on a regular schedule, regardless of its price. The investor may buy more shares when the price is low and fewer shares when the price is high.

In the same example above, suppose your stock goes down in value by 5%, but you believe this is just a temporary correction and not a continuous downtrend. You may decide you would like to add to your position to reap the net profit from the retracement. However, if you don't have enough capital, then you cannot buy these discounted shares. Many investors do this 'dollar cost averaging' periodically. If this is your strategy as well, adequate capital is necessary to reap the benefits.

Your Trading Goals

Your trading goals are an important factor in determining your capital requirement as well. For instance, if you are looking to create $100,000 per year in income through trading, this will require $1 Million if you are fortunate enough to create a 10% yield off your portfolio.

Margin Requirements

Margin trading allows you to leverage the assets in your account (cash and securities) to purchase more securities than you would be able to buy on a cash-only basis. You are trading with borrowed funds. Therefore, there is a potential for increased gains as well as increased losses.

If you decide the risk of margin loans is right for you, they can be a low-cost, flexible way to borrow funds for your trading strategy. This is especially true if you use a brokerage like Interactive Brokers which charges around 2.5% interest-- or less depending on the amount of capital you have. That sounds more cost effective than credit cards and most other types of lending.

Margin loans aren't for everyone. It presents many unique risks, with the biggest being losing more capital than your original investment. However, if you improve your money and risk management skills, margins can be used to increase your market exposure by providing fast access to cash at opportune times.

Margin Maintenance & Risks

Each broker requires an initial deposit to request margin privileges. For instance, Scottrade requires a low $2,000. Once a loan is extended, you're required to keep a minimum equity level. This is called the maintenance requirement.

The two biggest risks of margin trading are amplified losses and margin calls. Due to increased market exposure, it's possible to lose more funds than the initial capital deposited in your account. If that occurs, you won't just be responsible for paying back the loan. You will also have to pay the interest. Keep in mind interest rates may fluctuate during the time your loan is outstanding.

All brokers require you to keep a minimum equity level in your account at all times. If you fall below this minimum maintenance requirement, your broker may issue a margin call that requires you to deposit cash or close trades immediately. If you're unable to do either of these things, your broker may need to force the closing of some or all of your securities to bring your account back below the equity requirement.

When to Enter and Exit Trades

When deciding on when to enter a trade, it is important for an investor to get rid of all the noise and focus. Only then will an investor understand the prevailing trend and capitalize on it. While this book promotes investing in marijuana stocks for the long term, it is still important to familiarize yourself with the current trends so that you will maximize your profits. This is especially true considering all the volatility this sector has had and will have in the future.

Below is a list of general rules to entering and exiting trades that will help you find the greatest potential for profit with the lowest risk. There is always risks with trading in a burgeoning industry, but by sticking to these rules the chances of making successful trades suddenly turn in your favor. These rules take advantage of the fact that the market ebbs and flows in waves. Much of it is common sense, but beginning traders often do not listen to common sense and instead let their emotions dictate their choices.

1. When marijuana stocks are uptrending, buy the stronger companies. When marijuana stocks are downtrending, sell the weaker companies.

Why?

When the there is a pullback, a stronger stock's share price will not go down as much-- if at all. These are the same stocks to trade in an uptrend. Companies like Aphria Inc. and Canopy Growth Corp. are the current leaders of this sector and they are the ones that move the market higher, with minimal pullbacks.

For instance, when Trump's administration insinuated that they would take action against states that legalized recreational marijuana, cannabis stocks around the world deflated in share price. But Canadian Aphria Inc. barely moved compared to the rest. Why? This is likely due to investors knowing Aphria was one of the few cannabis companies that has continuous positive cash flow despite huge expansion projects. This is no small feat.

By the same token, an investor should short sell the weaker penny stocks when the marijuana stock market is downtrending. Short sell these stocks because they will likely drop in price more than the market. At the time of this writing, there is at least a few hundred marijuana stocks trading on markets around the world. Some of the stronger stocks of that bunch have been listed In this book. Therefore, there is plenty of riskier, smaller stocks out there perfect for short selling.

This strategy should provide more safety and relative outperformance profits. Keep in mind, since the list of relatively strong stocks and the list of relatively weak stocks can change periodically, it becomes necessary to study the companies in question using the principles touched upon in the last chapter.

2. Wait for the Pullback

With nearly all trends-- up or down, there are always pullbacks in the share price as day traders collect small profits. The market moves in waves for this reason, sometimes mysteriously. When studying an uptrending line on a chart, you may notice almost a staircase pattern, or in other words, higher highs and lower lows.

Therefore, it's often good practice to enter a long position after the price moves down toward the trendline and then moves back higher. In simplistic terms, buy at the beginning of the next upward wave to obtain more profits. Or if you are short selling, wait until the price moves up the downward sloping trendline and make your entry when the stock begins to move back down.

It is important for an investor to be patient with this type of strategy. However, a noticeable pullback may not come if a surging stock is hot enough. This is where your due diligence is required. If your research shows this trend is not slowing down, you may have to start a position as soon as you can. Researching the company with the principles outlined in the previous chapter will help an investor discern between a trend based on hype or a trend based on valid fundamentals.

Sometimes a pullback is more than just a pullback. It could be the start of a downward trend. Again, due diligence is required. It's usually wise practice to not add to a losing stock. However, its sudden spiral downward could be due to a correction in the whole sector and not because of anything wrong with the company. If this is the case, you will have more opportunities to obtain shares of the stock at discounted prices. This is why it is important to practice money management. In other words, do not use up all your capital every time you add to a position. If you do, you may not have enough to add to future positions when there are future pullbacks- big or small. Instead, add to your position with small doses of capital-- only if you believe a retracement will happen. This will result in an overall net profit.

3. Profit Taking

Unless your strategy is buy and hold, usually you will want to close a position before a correction occurs. Since markets move in waves in all time periods, it should be evident what a stock's previous highs and lows are. These are often used for reference when determining entry and exit points.

Therefore, the strategy with the lowest risk is this: if you have a long position and your stock is in an uptrend, take profits at the former price high. If you have a short position and your stock is in a downtrend, take profits at the former price low.

4. Buy at the Breakout

Keep in mind, the stocks in question in this book are growth stocks. Therefore, it is very likely these stocks could explode past their previous price highs. When a stock surges past its resistance point (prior price high) without slowing down, that is a pretty good indication it is on its way to a longer trend. Do your due diligence-- Find out why it's surging. If its fundamentals are relatively sound, you probably want to enter a position to see what new highs this stock might take you.

5. When low risk entries are not visible, step aside.

Traders should generally trade with the overall trend and patiently wait for low risk entries to make the odds of obtaining profit more likely. However, sometimes the signals to buy or sell are not obvious. If this is the case, you don't have to do anything. It's better to just step aside and wait for a more visible signal. Funny enough, this is often the most difficult thing for most investors to do. They often get too emotional. They feel the need to do something, which results in making bad decisions.

Conclusion- Cut Losses / Let Profits Run!

There is no such thing as a perfect strategy. Sometimes, a trading strategy will not be in tune with current market sentiment despite your carefully planned research. Consequently, your strategy may result in a string of consecutive losing trades. During these times, it is important you preserve working capital.

By managing your risk properly and preserving working capital, you can weather-these-storms. Proper risk management will control your losses in such a way to keep them manageable and not catastrophic. A catastrophic loss means you can't even continue to trade and recoup your losses. Don't let this happen to you!

In most trading strategies, the objective is not having the highest possible percentage of winning trades, but instead to trade profitably over a long term. In fact, some investors are quite profitable only winning 50% of their trades. Or even less. How? They cut their losses quickly, but they let their profits run as high as they may go. What really matters in the long run is that the sum total of profits is greater than the sum total of losses.

Sources

All of the factual information in this book, including stock statistics and government legislation, was compiled from a myriad of sources, including news media websites and websites compiling data for research. Below is a list that includes these sources.

It is recommended that readers of this book visit these websites, since stocks and government legislation could change from one moment to the next. To deepen your research further, use Google Alerts to monitor the web for up to the minute news on anything related to marijuana. To create a list of alerts, visit Google Alerts and in the box at the top, enter a topic you want to follow. Google will then send you an email when there are new results for your topic. These emails will arrive in your inbox as often as you like, and the topics you entered can be changed at any time.

www.seekingalpha.com - A crowd-sourced content service for financial markets, including stock market Insights & financial analysis, free earnings call transcripts, investment ideas and ETF & stock research, all written by finance experts.

www.bloomberg.com - Bloomberg delivers business and markets news, data, analysis, and video to the world, featuring stories from Businessweek and Bloomberg News.

www.investopedia.com - "Investopedia is the world's leading source of financial content on the web, ranging from market news to retirement strategies, investing education to insights from around the world."

www.thecannabist.co - Marijuana news and culture, research, resources, strain reviews, cannabutter recipes, vaporizer & cannabis concentrates info, hemp, Colorado dispensary map.

www.bezinga.com - Stock Market Quotes, Business News, Financial News, Trading Ideas, and Stock Research by Professionals.

www.theguardian.com - Billing itself as the world's leading liberal voice, the Guardian is a British daily newspaper with the latest world news, sports, business, opinion, analysis and reviews.

www.leafly.com - Leafly provides visitors with reviews of the best medical cannabis strains.

"Leafly is the largest cannabis website in the world, with over 10 million monthly visitors and 40 million page views across its website and mobile applications." - Wikipedia.org

www.cnn.com - View the latest news and breaking news today for U.S., world, weather, entertainment, politics and health at CNN.com.

"The Cable News Network is an American basic cable and satellite television news channel owned by the Turner Broadcasting System division of Time Warner. It was founded in 1980 by American media proprietor Ted Turner as a 24-hour cable news channel." - Wikipedia.org

www.naturalnews.com - Independent News on Natural Health and the World. Natural News is a science-based natural health advocacy organization led by activist-turned-scientist Mike Adams, the Health Ranger.

www.marijuanastocks.com - "Our goal is to become the central hub for all who are seeking current Marijuana Stock News as well as cannabis industry, political and social news, articles, trends & overall insight, delivered in a way that we all can relate to."

www.cnbc.com - Latest business news on stock markets, financial & earnings. View world markets streaming charts & video; check stock tickers and quotes.

www.fool.com - The Motley Fool is a multimedia financial-services company that provides leading insight and analysis about stocks, investing, and personal finance services.

www.newcannabisventures.com - Contributing original content and curating quality news on only the most promising cannabis companies and the most influential investors, allowing you to save time as you stay on top of the latest trends in this dynamic industry.

www.insiderfinancial.com - Insider Financial offers stock news & analysis on U.S. equities.

www.streetregister.com – Wall Street Financial News and Analyst Insights.

"Our mission is to provide unmatched news and insight on newsworthy and momentum stocks for traders and investors. At Street Register we believe that there are plenty of emerging growth companies across a variety of industry sectors with plenty of hidden value. Market discovery and innovation often occurs in small to mid-size companies that are either misunderstood or underrepresented. We focus on identifying these companies and uncovering their stories before the rest of the market to ensure that you receive the full story – every single day."

www.nytimes.com - Breaking news, multimedia, reviews & opinion on Washington, business, sports, movies, travel, books, jobs, education, real estate and financial markets.

www.forbes.com - Forbes is an American business magazine focused on original articles about business, investing, technology, entrepreneurship, leadership, and lifestyle.

www.merryjane.com - "Merry Jane is the definitive cannabis resource offering exclusive content and relatable perspectives on culture, news, video, food, and style."

www.nasdaq.com - Named after the second-largest exchange in the world by market capitalization, the Nasdaq Stock Market website features stock quotes and analysis.

www.newswire.ca - Cited as the most-referenced source of Canadian news releases for journalists, Canada Newswire engages with audiences across the globe.

Conclusion

We certainly hope you enjoyed reading "International Marijuana" as much as we enjoyed writing it. The effort and opportunity in researching and writing this book has been an enriching experience for everyone involved. Not to mention, it even deepened our own understanding of the industry and made our own investment choices even clearer.

Remember, as with most books about stocks, some of the material will become dated with time. This is why we also included chapters meant to teach investors how to research companies as fundamentals and the industry changes.

Finally, if you enjoyed this book, please take the time to share your thoughts and post a review. It would be greatly appreciated.